TOAST

TOAST

FINDING FREEDOM IN THE KITCHEN

by kara elise

PHOTOGRAPHS BY PAPER ANTLER

ISBN 978-0-692-93512-5

Photographed by Paper Antler
Designed by Hanna Snyder

Printed in the USA
First printing, September 2017

www.bykaraelise.com

CONTENTS

CONTENTS

SAVORY

CONTENTS

FREEDOM

My friends call me the "what's-in-your kitchen" expert. Admittedly, I love a lot of things about food... but one of my favorites is coming into a friend's kitchen, taking inventory of what's there, and making a surprising creation from the unusual combo of leftovers they have around.

I learned this skill very young. My mom was the best at it. As a mother of five with limited income, she'd walk into the kitchen, look at what we had, and create something delicious with the bits and pieces she found.

I call this gift "food intuition". It's the ability to think about the ingredients in front of you and find a way to use them resourcefully.

Whenever I have the opportunity to make food for someone, it is a chance to get to know them a little better. In addition to being known for resourcefulness in the kitchen, I'm also known as the one who loves "all the feels". I deeply cherish conversation and relationships, so for me a meal is more about the person sitting across from me than the meal itself. Because while I value good food, I value people more.

Eating a meal together simply creates a space for relationships to thrive. The dinner table is a great example of this. It's a place to gather, sit presently with the people around you, and communally nourish your bodies. However, the world of food can be intimidating. Hosting can create stress and anxiety due to the anticipation of "what should I make!?" Often, many people feel ill-equipped in the kitchen from the expectation to create something magical. Through hosting various dinner parties and events, I discovered that toast is a simple, beautiful solution to this.

Here is the truth about toast... It is one of the easiest foods to be resourceful with. I often keep a loaf of bread in my freezer, and get quite creative with whatever I find in my kitchen to craft some yummy toasts. Regardless of your dietary restrictions, there are endless types of bread you can play with! I tend to stock up on a loaf of ciabatta (a favorite of mine) and a loaf of gluten-free bread to have at my fingertips. With a few more ingredients that you likely already have in your kitchen, you can quickly create something beautiful and delicious.

Hosting is my love language. Many times, if a friend stops in, I love having the freedom to offer some form of nourishment - usually in the form of a toast. Food creates space. It creates space for authentic conversation and connection. It allows us to slow down and be present with another person. Keeping it simple with toasts allows this to be possible everyday.

So, my hope is that this book inspires you with fresh ideas for your own meals to share. The truth is, anyone can make toast! Whether you have five minutes and only a few ingredients, or you feel like getting fancy, there is a toast for every person and occasion. I will give you tips on how to think freely and intuitively for when you're crafting something elaborate with friends and family, or simply just taking a moment to nourish yourself.

INTUITION

I often think about how the kitchen is a metaphor for life. In all its beauty, life is incredibly messy. It can be gritty and unexpected. As people, we are constantly processing, moving with the flow, and responding to the circumstances life brings us. Each time we're thrown a curve ball, we can choose to fully engage by slowing down and noticing what the discomfort evokes in us. Then, we have the option to either run from a difficult time, or turn the mess into something beautiful. We can create beauty out of the inevitable disorder and chaos we're presented with.

Like bread that must be kneaded and left to rise over and over again; such is the very nature of the seasons. Of the days and months and years we walk through. Without the kneading and rising, the dough would be tough - not the delightful, crusty bread we hope to bite into.

When I was 13, I fell in love with the kitchen. This mostly happened because our family was going through a very large mess. We experienced something that shattered normality for us and created massive amounts of pain. As the middle of five children, I felt immense pressure to keep it together. With a limited awareness at such a young age of how to process emotion, the kitchen became a place of tactile therapy for me. I would spend hours baking and cooking. Creating something outside of myself like this helped to calm the pain that was happening inside. I let myself create messes in the kitchen because they were transformed into a final product that was beautiful and delicious.

I began making toasts out of convenience. They were a meal that I could quickly assemble and still get creative with. Not to mention, I have always been the girl who loves bread. Bread and butter are probably the most comforting things to me, and an innocent reminder of childhood. While clearing the table at home, I'd often sneak swipes of butter from the dish. My parents eventually had to remove it before I started cleaning up, or whole sticks of butter might go missing.

In my early 20s, I worked in residence life during my time in grad school. Each month, I would host dinner for a group of my student leaders, and I found myself wanting to get more and more creative with the meals. It was a fun challenge to me - to create something for others.

Because food is just that. It's an art form. It's truly creative.

Yet at the same time, it's so freeing. Food as art is a practice you can't take too seriously, because you create it only to consume it. You inevitably destroy it.

Those years of hosting in grad school are when I fell in love with welcoming people into my home for dinner. A few years later, after being worn out from Chicago and craving a new pace of life, I decided to move to Los Angeles.

It was impulsive and hilarious as I look back. I had no money, no job, and no place to live. However, I had friends, and I knew that community was the most important thing for me in that season. In May of 2013

I packed up my life, and like many typical LA stories, I headed to the West Coast as a dreamer, full of wonder and ideation.

While driving me across the country, my best friend Michelle asked, "If money never mattered and you didn't need to make a dollar, what would you want to do with your life?"

"Have people over for dinner," I told her.

And that was it.

Having people over. For dinner.

Having people over was the heart and drive, and dinner was the vehicle to do so.

When I arrived in LA, I began telling everyone, "I'm going to have a dinner party company." I am someone who believes so much in the power of our words. That what we speak propels us forward in life. When we declare our dreams, it gives us the ability to walk into them. But when we speak our fears and limitations, we become bound by them.

Quite quickly, I started to book small dinner parties. An anniversary party here, a birthday party there, etc. I was cooking for groups of 12-16 people, creating spaces for them to connect over good food and drink. It made me come alive.

Shortly after, I miraculously moved into a loft in downtown. On the second night there, I was sitting on the floor with my friend Heidi, drinking whiskey. "We should invite people over to drink whiskey with us," I said. (Heidi and I are both high extroverts who love the thought of meeting strangers.) "I will cook for them, and we'll host dinner parties with new people each month!"

It was this night that we came up with the idea of "Whiskey Wednesdays", a bi-monthly dinner party for strangers. The concept was simple, but the heart of it was for people to connect around food and drink in an authentic, genuine way. In a city like Los Angeles, where time is precious, pretense is heightened, and life is chaotic, this kind of REAL connection is rare.

So I began Whiskey Wednesdays.

If you've met me or had dinner with me, you know I love intentional questions. I so enjoy understanding people, the way they're wired, and what makes them tick. At each Whiskey Wednesday, we introduced new table questions. In many ways, they became the mantra of each dinner as a practical way of engaging the entire table. Sometimes the questions were simple and funny, like your worst date or how you dressed in middle school. Other times, the questions dove deeply into what we were hoping or longing for in that season.

These kinds of questions are powerful. Not only because they create conversation, but also because they have the ability to give us insight into one another in an unconventional, non-threatening way. If I ask you about your favorite childhood vacation, you're actually revealing a deeper truth to me about what shaped you, what you value, how you experience fun, and so on. When you do that with a group of strangers, it's so bonding. You instantly create meaningful connections with people you've just met.

Many friendships, partnerships, and even dates came out of Whiskey Wednesdays! I was once at a rooftop concert in Hollywood, and the spoken word poet there asked the crowd if anyone was in love. This darling couple in front of me raised their hands giddily and shared the most adorable, love-filled kiss when they announced their love to the crowd. At the end of the show, while I was talking with friends, they turned around to me. "Are you Kara?" they asked. Instantly, I recognized them from nearly a year back.

"We met at your loft at a Whiskey Wednesday!" they excitedly told me, and went on to tell me their story of falling in love after that evening of communal conversation.

I nearly died from excitement. In that moment, I felt like everything I was doing made complete sense to me. Food is a universal language that we all share. By hosting people with it, I was able to create a space for true connection.

I continue to host Whiskey Wednesdays, and toasts have become a regular part of the dinners. Here's why: when I began cooking for that many people every other week, it was quite a lot to manage. Hosting a dinner party can be paralyzing, but I created Whiskey Wednesdays because I wanted to be able to truly HOST. If I was too stressed about preparing the meal, I noticed that it negatively affected the environment and experience of my guests. In an effort to ease the mental strain, I came up with a meal formula.

Protein. Salad. Side. Toast.

That was it. You figure out a main protein dish, you choose a really good accompanying salad and side, and then you make a toast that takes the meal to the next level.

Toasts are a dish you can even make ahead of time. They can be prepared on a baking sheet and popped in the oven right before serving. Plus, they can turn out really beautiful - and so much of the joy of eating is celebrating the beauty in front of you.

Toasts have become a signature of mine, and often are the conversation of my dinner parties. Guests always say they love the way I unexpectedly put sweet potato on bread, play with various textures, and use a surprising combination of ingredients and colors.

My friends ask for them, my clients ask for them, and I guarantee once you get on the toast train you won't get off.

It's also important to note that toasts are inexpensive. They are a great thing to make when you're on a budget because of their versatility. Throughout this book, I really encourage you to think intuitively if you don't have one of the ingredients listed. You can see my substitution tips on page 17, but feel free to play with what is already in your kitchen. If you don't have asparagus, try broccoli! If you don't have a sweet potato, try using squash or beets! Don't have tahini? Try using another cream based sauce. You can even make your own with Greek yogurt!

Of course, I want to get you jazzed about toast. But more than anything, I want to teach you freedom in the kitchen. Freedom to not get it right, but simply play, listen to your intuition, and learn.

When I hear people say they can't cook, it breaks my heart. Because you absolutely can. Toast is the walking of sports. We can all do it. Once you get a bit more fit, you can try jogging. And then before you know it, you're running marathons. Like anything, cooking may come more naturally to some of us, but we can all participate and enjoy it.

So dive in. Make some good food. And get creative; it's the only way to do the kitchen.

PLAY

I'm a massive fan of personality tests and assessments. In grad school I studied the Myers-Briggs, StrengthsFinder, and the Enneagram. I have this theory that so much of who we are is reflected in how we cook. The way we approach life can be revealed in the very way we assemble a meal.

I met my friend Lindsey during my first year in LA. We were both part of "girls group"; a weekly meeting of women in Los Angeles to discuss matters of the heart. Lindsey quickly became a dear friend, and she'd often come over for breakfast, lunch, or dinner. I found myself always making toasts for her.

After a while, Lindsey kept asking me for recipes. But the funny thing is, I don't really use recipes, so I had a hard time giving her specifics.

"Use your intuition," I'd tell her. However, this statement actually infuriated her, because the language of food was still one that she was learning.

Fast forward a couple of years, and Lindsey had moved to Northern California. She called me one night in a panic and said she was having people over for dinner. She was currently at Trader Joe's and she needed a Kara consultation for what to buy. I walked her through a few shopping tips, gave her some ideas for easy, dinner-party-friendly meals, and told her, "Make a toast."

"HOW?" she asked.

I explained that just like anything, it always begins with the foundation. Start with good quality bread.

Secondly, think about what your palate is craving. Next, what else are you cooking? What flavors in your meal can your toast complement? Ultimately toast is neutral, but you can transform it to become the highlight (or the entirety!) of your meal.

So Lindsey starts making toasts. And it becomes her jam. Pardon the pun.

She starts thinking creatively about flavor combinations, what fruits match with cheese, which sauces complement avocado, and what seasonings taste good with a roast chicken dish. In her exploration of toasts, she begins to learn the language of food.

Toasts taught Lindsey to play. To be free in the kitchen. To let go of what she didn't know, and dive into thinking about food in a new way.

That is why I love toast. Because it's not formulaic. It is so approachable, and it's FUN.

Have fun with this book. Get a little messy and playful. Think differently about food and flavors. Ultimately, get a little more free in the kitchen.

THE BASICS

TOASTING TIPS

There are many ways to toast bread! Your options are endless. Below are a few of my most frequent toasting techniques.

OVEN
Preheat your oven to 400°. Place your toasts on a baking sheet and drizzle with olive oil. Toast for 6-10 minutes, or until the toasts are golden.

TOASTER
Toasting 101! Just pop those slices in a toaster and let them get golden.

SKILLET
Heat a skillet on medium-high heat. Add a bit of olive oil and then toast your bread in it until the slices are golden on each side.

GRILL
Have a grill? Spread a bit of oil on each side of your bread and grill for a minute or two on each side, or until the bread is toasty.

SIMPLE SUBSTITUTIONS

When we cook, we often think literally about ingredients. At times, a structured recipe is necessary, but the fun of toast is that it's fully free. As you create a toast, I encourage you to think about what else could be added, substituted, and used to vary up the flavor. Below are a couple of options for substitutions, but I encourage you to think outside of the box. If you don't have whipped feta for example, what other cheese could give you that very salty and cream-like flavor? If you don't have strawberries, do you think that raspberries might give the same effect? What kind of greens are you actually craving? Kale, spinach, or maybe a local arugula?

SQUASH
Squash is a versatile food, so you can swap out butternut for acorn, etc. If you don't have squash, try using something with a similar texture like beets, sweet potatoes, or smashed chickpeas.

BERRIES
Berries are best when in season! If you can't find a seasonal berry to match the recipe, try using frozen berries or even different, in-season fruits to mix up the flavor combos.

CHEESE
Cheeses are fun to experiment with. Want a sharper flavor on your toast? Use a gorgonzola or a blue

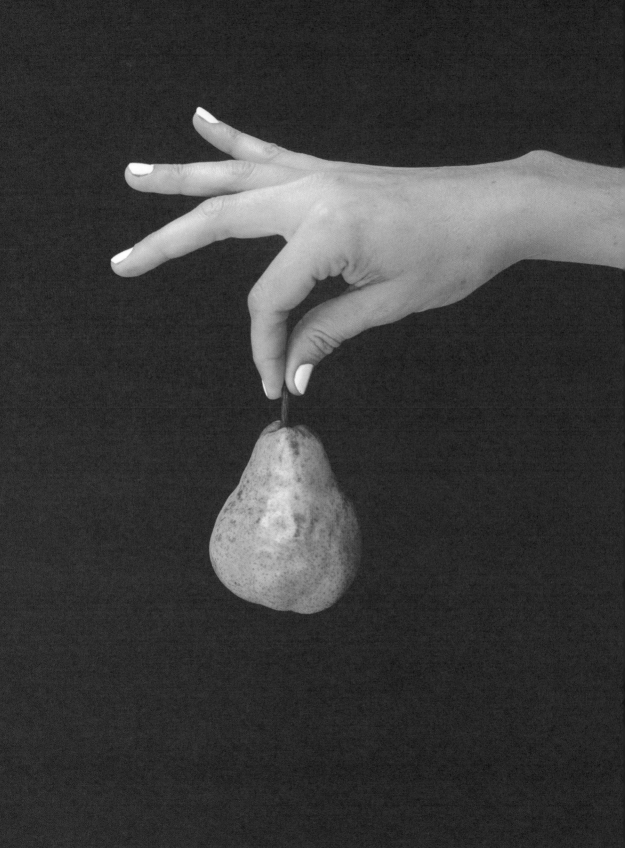

cheese. Want a salty flavor? Use feta or a sharp cheddar. Don't have cream cheese? Swap out for a goat cheese or even ricotta!

GREENS
Greens are also an easy interchange. I love the flavor of kale, but perhaps you prefer Swiss chard! You can vary up greens based on the texture and flavor you're looking to achieve.

BREAD

The great thing about toast is that your bread choices are endless. I love buying local, scouring my farmers markets for new varieties of fresh baked bread. I also tend to buy a couple loaves and freeze them so that I always have options on hand. Throughout the recipes I've suggested some options for you to use, but the truth is that you can use anything! Bread is versatile, so play with flavor and don't be afraid to try a new combination! Plus, if you're gluten-free, toasts can still be on your menu! Some of my favorite toasts come on gluten-free bread because of its spongy, delicious texture.

MY GO-TOS
Ciabatta, rye, whole grain, sourdough, Sperlonga, simple sandwich bread, gluten-free bread (I love Udi's!), and French baguettes.

EGGS

Oh the infamous egg. He's delicious and versatile and yet sometimes tricky to get right. While my toast recipes for you are quite simple, they can seem intimidating if you're not empowered with the basics. Below are some instructions on egg cooking techniques. With these tips, you'll have everything you need to craft your perfect toast.

SOFT BOILED
To make the perfect soft boil, let your water come to a rolling boil. Lower the heat and let the water reduce to a rapid simmer. Gently lower the eggs into the water one at a time. Cook the eggs for 5 to 7 minutes. For 1 to 2 eggs, cook 5 minutes for a very runny yolk, or up to 7 minutes for a barely-set yolk.

HARD BOILED
For the perfect hard boil, place eggs in large saucepan in a single layer. Add cold water to cover eggs by 1 inch. Bring your water to a boil over high heat, then remove from the burner. Cover your pan and let your eggs sit in the hot water for about 12 minutes. Drain and serve warm, or cool completely under cold water and refrigerate.

POACHED
Poaching an egg can be so intimidating, but when you get it right, it is so darn delicious. To begin, fill a saucepan with a few inches of water and bring to a boil. Then, turn the water down to a small simmer. You'll see bubbles surfacing, but you don't want the water rolling. Next, crack the egg into a small cup. This will let you gently ease the egg into the water. Add 1 teaspoon vinegar to the water to help keep the egg intact. I like to give my simmering water a swirl, then slowly ease the egg in. Cook the egg for 4 minutes, then use a slotted spoon to scoop the egg out and let it drain a bit. Gently place your egg on top of your toast, or set aside until your toast is assembled and ready.

FRIED
For the perfect fried egg, I like to heat a frying pan on high heat with a dash of olive oil for about 2 minutes. Then, gently crack the egg onto the pan. Cover with a lid and turn your heat to medium for 1-2 minutes. Then, turn off your heat completely and let the egg continue to cook for about 3 minutes, or until the whites

are set and the yolk is runny.

SOFT-SCRAMBLED
Whisk together your eggs in a small bowl with 1-2 teaspoons of milk (non-dairy works as well). This is optional, but it adds a fluff to the eggs that is so yummy. Heat a frying pan on medium with a pat of butter or a bit of olive oil for about 1 minute. Pour in the egg mixture and let it stand in the skillet briefly, just 30 to 60 seconds, to set the edges. Using a rubber spatula, stir slowly, folding the cooked and uncooked portions together. Continue to stir and cook slowly until the majority of the eggs are set.

SAUCES + SPICES

Sauces and spices are my love language. Truthfully, I think I eat toast half of the time because it's a vehicle for a condiment or sauce. Below are a few of my favorite go-to sauces and seasonings that you'll find throughout the recipes.

WHIPPED FETA
You'll need 8 ounces of crumbled feta cheese and 3 ounces of whipped cream cheese, both at room temperature. In a food processor, add your feta and pulse until crumbly. Scrape down the sides, then add in your cream cheese. Pulse until the mixture is creamy and fluffy.

PESTOS
I love making my own pestos! A combination of basil, olive oil, garlic, Parmesan, and some kind of nut is your basic recipe. You can use pine nuts, pistachios, walnuts, or any other nut to create a unique flavor. Throw about 1 cup olive oil, a large handful of basil, 2 garlic cloves, ¼ cup Parmesan, ¼ cup nuts, and some sea salt into a blender or Vitamix, and you've got a deliciously perfect homemade pesto to use on your toasts. If you're dairy-free, omit the Parmesan!

SALT
This is common sense, but salt is the spice of life. Maldon Sea Salt is my ultimate favorite with its sharp texture and delicious crunch. Flavored salts from Hepp's are also an absolute delight. Their truffle salt and Sriracha salt are always stocked in my pantry. My favorite zaatar, rosemary salt, and chili salt are from Ottolenghi - he's a genius of food and has inspired so much of my cooking.

GOOD OLIVE OILS
This is essential to toast. I like a robust, golden olive oil with strong flavor. You can also experiment with flavored olive oils, like garlic infused or truffle oil.

HEMP SEEDS
I love keeping these around for toasts because they add a delicious, crunchy texture and have amazing health benefits. These seeds are packed with fiber, protein, and healthy Omega-3s to promote brain and heart health.

TAHINI
My love of Middle Eastern food has given me daily cravings for tahini. I keep a jar in my refrigerator at all times. To make a delicious tahini sauce, mix 2 tablespoons tahini with some sea salt, a dash of honey, and a bit of water. Whisk until it's your desired consistency, and you're good to go!

EVERYTHING BUT THE BAGEL
I discovered this seasoning at Trader Joe's a while back and it is remarkable. If you don't have a Trader Joe's nearby or can't find the mixture, the seasoning is simply a combination of sesame seeds (both black and white), dried minced garlic, sea salt, and dried minced onion. You can easily make your own batch!

SUNRISE

Breakkie! Where do I even begin? It's my favorite meal, my stabilizing routine, the best way to start my day. I actually go to bed thinking about what I'm going to have for breakfast. The flavors are abundant, the options endless, and the nourishment necessary.

I'm an incredibly fast paced human. I come from a family of five children, and my mom is an active woman who has passed her energy and zest for life off to me. In addition, being a single woman in your 30s in Los Angeles often means you have to hustle. In general, I wake up in the morning with a complete awareness of the 900 things that must happen in that day. When I moved here in 2013, I made a commitment to slow down and "host" myself, or someone else, everyday for breakfast. It has become a practice, both emotionally and spiritually, to pause, to be, and to get nourished. It's not just about breakkie, or the food even. It's about what is created when you choose to prioritize your well-being.

My sunrise challenge to you is this: slow down. Linger over something you create. Notice the way sitting still and being present with yourself orients the entirety of your day. Remember, you are worth your time.

MIXED BERRY + GOAT CHEESE + HEMP + LIME

Are you ready for a flavor explosion? When I was 21, my best friend Michelle and I quit our minimum wage coffee shop jobs and went down to Costa Rica for three weeks. It was an epic adventure for us, full of laughter, hitch hiking, and very dangerous cliff jumping. Costa Rica has incredible food, and one thing they do especially well? Zest. Yes, ZEST. Lime, lemon, and orange zest were used on so many dishes. The added colors and flavors were delightful! I returned inspired, and began adding zest to my dishes. The lime zest on this toast adds such dimension. The sweet berry flavors, tangy lime, and crunchy hemp seed are a winning trio. Plus, the hemp adds protein, and you'll get loads of vitamins from the fruit!

1 large slice good bread, I'm using multigrain

8 blackberries, sliced lengthwise

2 large strawberries, sliced

1 large Tbsp goat cheese

2 tsp hemp seed

Zest of one lime

Drizzle of olive oil, optional

Preheat your oven to 375°. Spread your bread with goat cheese, then layer with your berries. Drizzle with olive oil (optional). Toast in the oven for 10 minutes, or until the edges of your toast are golden. Remove from the oven and sprinkle with hemp seeds and lime zest!

TIP: Don't have a lime? Try a lemon! I like to squeeze a bit of lime juice on the toast as well for an extra citrus kick.

Makes 1 slice

AVOCADO + POMEGRANATE + TAHINI + MICROGREENS

In Chicago, I used to frequent a falafel shop that had the most delicious tahini. Tahini is a condiment made from toasted sesame seeds. After discovering its flavor, I've found ways to use it in so many dishes. It's a go to flavor of mine for dressings and sauces. Tahini on toast is a win because it immediately adds a velvety richness. Coupled with the mildness of the avocado and the sweetness of the pomegranate, this toast packs a full spectrum of flavor all in one bite.

2 slices good bread

½ avocado

2 Tbsp tahini

½ tsp salt

2 Tbsp pomegranate seeds

Microgreens

Honey to drizzle, optional

Toast your bread! Thinly slice your avocado and spritz with lemon, or another citrus, to keep it from going brown. Spread each slice with 1 tablespoon tahini. Top the tahini with sliced avocado, pomegranate, and microgreens. Add salt and an optional drizzle of honey.

TIP: Microgreens are great for color and add an extra nutrient bump in the morning. If you don't have them, try adding another green like arugula, chopped parsley, or basil for some more nutritional value. If tahini isn't your flavor of choice, not to worry! Try using hummus instead.

Makes 2 slices

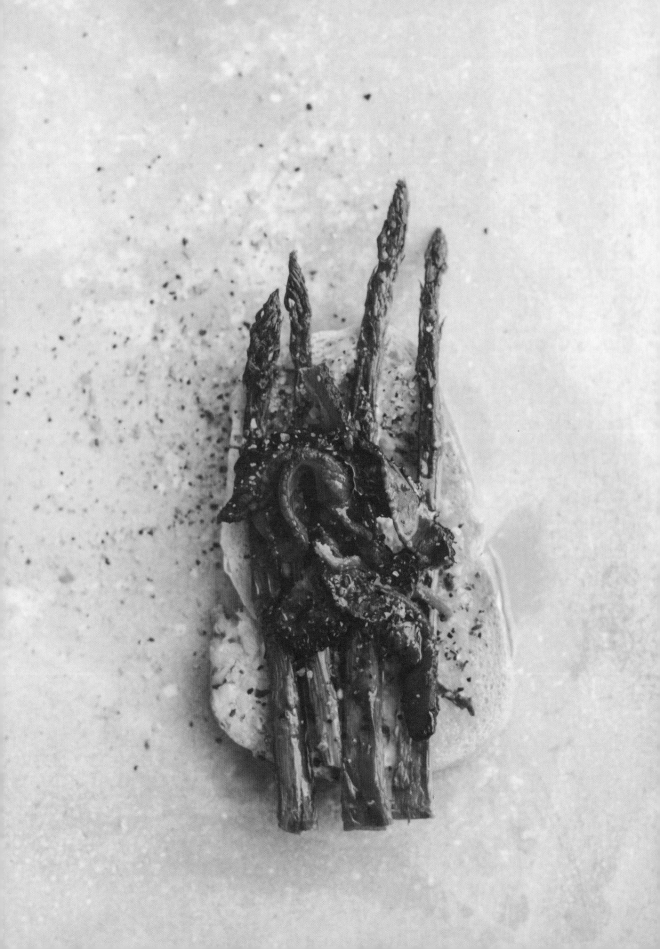

CHARRED ASPARAGUS + BACON + OLIVE OIL

I discovered this toast after hosting a dinner party one evening. I woke up the next day with a pile of dishes and loads of work, and couldn't really be bothered to make something for myself. But! I looked in the refrigerator and had leftover asparagus that I had roasted the night before, bacon that had been used in a sauce, and some bread! So I simply assembled. And truthfully it was delicious. I now make this toast on the regular. If I'm making asparagus for dinner, I'll intentionally set some aside so I can create this toast seamlessly in the morning.

2 slices good bread

2-3 strips cooked bacon

8-10 spears roasted asparagus

2 Tbsp olive oil

2 tsp seasoning

Preheat your oven to 400°. Place your sliced bread on a baking sheet. Arrange your asparagus evenly among the two slices of bread. Top with your bacon. Drizzle your toasts liberally with olive oil. Add your seasoning of choice, then bake for 8-12 minutes, or until the edges of your asparagus begin to char.

TIP: If your asparagus isn't already roasted, you can roast it in the oven at 450° for 12 minutes with some olive oil, or you can char it in a cast iron skillet.

Makes 2 slices

KIWI + COCONUT + RICOTTA + FLAX + HONEY

Food has an incredible power to evoke memories within us. This toast, packed with tropical flavors, always seems to stir up memories of vacation in me. At times when I'm craving a getaway, it's the perfect thing to bite into. Enjoy it leisurely as a weekend breakfast, and daydream of all the lovely places in the world there are to visit. It's tropical, fruity, and the creamy goodness of the ricotta makes for a decadent morning treat. Plus, the flaxseed adds an amazing crunch and additional health benefits that start a day well.

4 slices good bread, I'm using multigrain

2 kiwis

¼ cup ricotta

2 Tbsp golden flaxseed

2 Tbsp coconut

Honey

Peel and slice your kiwis. Toast your slices of bread either in a toaster, the oven, or a pan. Once golden, spread each slice with 1 tablespoon ricotta. Layer the slices of kiwi along each toast. Top the kiwi slices with flaxseed and coconut. Liberally drizzle each toast with about ½ tablespoon honey.

TIP: One of my consistent morning drinks is a matcha latte. The flavors of matcha go so well with this toast, and the colors match! To make a matcha latte: Place 1 teaspoon matcha powder in your mug. Top with a splash of nearly boiling water and whisk vigorously until the matcha is completely dissolved (use a micro whisk if you have one!). Add in 1 teaspoon honey and a dash of vanilla extract. Whisk again. Then, top the entire mixture with steamed almond milk. It is oh-so delicious.

Makes 4 slices

BERRY + COCONUT + HONEY

I call these my "lay by the pool" toasts. In Los Angeles, the weather is always quite warm and dreamy. I don't take advantage of the lovely pool at my loft often enough, but when I do, I love bringing down a snack, reading a book, and then taking a nice dip in the water. There is something so summery about these delicious little toasts. They're great for mornings when you have a little extra time to linger and indulge. Rich in color and packed with calcium, potassium, magnesium, and electrolytes from the coconut, they'll start your morning well with good fuel.

2 slices good bread, try a French baguette to make minis

½ cup choice of berries

2 Tbsp unsweetened flaked coconut

1 Tbsp honey

1 Tbsp coconut oil

Preheat your oven to 375˚. Place your bread on a baking sheet and spread each piece with a bit of coconut oil. Chop your berries and add evenly on each slice. Top with coconut. Drizzle with honey and bake for 8-10 minutes, or until your coconut is golden!

TIP: I like adding cinnamon to these on occasion for an even richer flavor. If you're a coffee drinker, these taste delicious with a coconut milk latte!

Makes 2 slices

POMEGRANATE + LOX

My dear friend Sarah runs a beautiful and culture-changing women's magazine called Darling. It is a publication intent on changing the way women see and feel about themselves. Along with the print magazine, they host many events around the country to create community among women. I remember the first time I got to host a Darling Brunch I was so nervous and wanted everything to be perfect. I made these gorgeous lox toasts because of their beauty and vibrancy. They are not only ridiculously beautiful, but are also packed with incredible, clean ingredients that leave you feeling lovely on the inside too. This recipe makes 8 toasts so you can host your own color-packed brunch!

8 slices good rye bread

4 eggs, soft boiled (see page 20)

Olive oil

8 Tbsp cream cheese

½ red onion

2 radishes

1 Persian cucumber

4 oz quality smoked salmon

4 sprigs dill

¼ cup pomegranate seeds

Preheat your oven to 375°. Arrange the slices of rye bread on a baking sheet. Drizzle the bread lightly with olive oil and toast in the oven for about 10 minutes. While the toasts are in the oven, thinly slice your onion, radish, and cucumber. Remove the baking sheet from the oven, and spread each slice with 1 tablespoon cream cheese. Distribute the salmon among the toasts, then follow with the onion, radish, and cucumber. Slice the soft boiled eggs in half, then top each toast with half an egg. Lastly, sprinkle each toast with pomegranate seeds and small sprigs of dill.

TIP: These toasts are fine to make ahead of time! They don't need to be warm. I love making them an hour or so before I have guests over so they're ready to go when my friends walk in the door!

Makes 8 slices

GOAT CHEESE + BERRY + HONEY STUFFED FRENCH TOAST

Of all the Sunrise toasts, this is the most indulgent. I discovered stuffed french toast accidentally at a grilled cheese dinner party. I was crafting a goat cheese grilled cheese and threw in some berries. Immediately, I loved the flavor combo. The next morning, I just had to try to recreate the deliciousness in a french toast version. Packed with goat cheese, honey, berries, and topped with even more honey and a dash of brown sugar, this toast is the ultimate weekend brunch that will leave you feeling a bit of breakfast euphoria.

4 slices good bread, I'm using whole wheat sandwich bread

2 oz goat cheese

½ cup red berries

4 Tbsp honey, divided

1 egg

⅓ cup milk

1 tsp cinnamon

1 tsp nutmeg

1 Tbsp butter

Brown sugar, optional

Begin by assembling your "sandwiches". Top 2 slices of bread with 1 ounce goat cheese, 1 tablespoon honey, and ¼ cup chopped berries each. Top with the other slices of bread to make a sandwich. In a shallow dish, whisk your egg, milk, and sugar. Heat a skillet on medium-high heat and add your butter. Dip each sandwich into the egg mixture, evenly coating each side, and allowing the mixture to seep in a bit.

When your butter is sizzling, add your stuffed bread to the skillet and fry on each side until golden (about 3 minutes per side). Remove from the heat and place each toast on a plate. Cut in half and stack diagonally. Drizzle each piece with the remaining honey, and top with a dash of brown sugar.

TIP: You can actually prepare these the night before, and then in the morning either fry them on a skillet or bake them in the oven at 350° for 25-30 minutes, or until the egg mixture is cooked through.

Makes 2 stuffed slices

BACON + CHIVE + SOFT SCRAMBLED EGGS

I have 4 siblings, and the youngest of the family is Jonathan. He is an amazing human, and even though he's six years younger than me, I have always felt that he has this innate maturity and ability to hold meaningful, life-giving conversations. As the baby of the siblings, he has always made us laugh. There is a beautiful simplicity to him that is foundational in our family. Jonathan has always liked simple food: a bacon and eggs kind of guy. This toast reminds me of him - it's the staples. The scrambled egg. The bacon. The hearty and filling breakfast that is easy and delicious. I like adding a little chive to give it a kick of extra flavor for any morning.

2 slices hearty, whole grain bread

3 eggs, soft scrambled (see page 21)

2 slices bacon

A few chives, chopped

Salt + pepper

Cook your bacon in a frying pan on medium-high heat until it reaches your desired crispiness. Set the bacon aside on a paper towel to absorb any extra grease. Soft scramble your eggs. Toast your bread in a toaster or any way you prefer. Top each slice of toast with the soft scrambled eggs. Crumble your bacon slices on top of each toast, then sprinkle with chopped chives. Finish with a dash of salt and pepper!

TIP: I'm such a condiment person, so I love adding extra sauce to any toast. Try mixing a dash of Sriracha with 1 tablespoon Greek yogurt for a creamy and spicy dipping sauce.

Makes 2 slices

STRAWBERRY + FIG JAM + GRANOLA + TOASTED COCONUT

For mornings when I wake up craving something sweet and crunchy, this toast is a must. I found this amazing granola at Trader Joe's that is packed with flax, chia, and so many good things. After eating a bowl of it, I immediately thought, this must go on toast! The combo of fig, berry, and coconut is so naturally delicious, and when you add a bit of crunch with the granola, it gets grand. I make two of these for myself in the morning along with an almond milk latte; it seems to make life a little more complete.

2 slices good bread

½ cup sliced Strawberries, or any berry of your choice

½ cup granola

½ cup flaked coconut

2 Tbsp Fig Jam, or jam of your choice

Honey to drizzle

Preheat your oven to 375° and place your bread on a baking sheet. I like to drizzle my slices with a dash of olive oil or a couple sprays of coconut oil. This gives them a bit of extra flavor and makes for a crunchier toast. Top each slice with 1 tablespoon fig jam, berries, granola, and coconut. Drizzle lightly with honey. Bake in your oven for 8-10 minutes, or until the coconut is golden. Serve warm.

TIP: While all toasts can be made on gluten-free bread, this one is especially delicious on a spongy rice bread and with gluten-free granola.

Makes 2 slices

RAW HONEY + RICOTTA + BANANA + CINNAMON + LEMON ZEST

Oh the banana. It's so good, isn't it? Last year, I found myself lacking motivation to work out, so I began working with a personal trainer. I had many preconceived notions around personal training, but what began with skepticism turned into a very transformative experience for me. My trainer shifted my views on fitness, offered me a new perspective on working out, and created a sense of encouragement around an area that I had been quite discouraged in. After a training session, I found myself craving potassium (great for bone and muscle health!), and the banana is a great way to get it. These toasts became a consistent post-workout snack for me, offering a refreshing, citrus bite that brings a burst of energy to any morning.

---

2 slices good bread, try a whole grain or spongy bread

1 banana, sliced as you like

2 heaping Tbsp ricotta

2 Tbsp raw honey

2 tsp cinnamon

Zest of one lemon

Toast the slices of bread. Spread your raw honey on each slice. Top the honey with ricotta and spread evenly. Add half of the sliced banana to each toast. Sprinkle with cinnamon and lemon zest!

TIP: If you're avoiding dairy, omit the ricotta for a non-dairy yogurt or a vegan cream cheese.

Makes 2 slices

PESTO + PARMESAN + A SOFT BOILED EGG

I used to think of pesto as a dinner flavor. I was accustomed to only using it in pastas and on pizzas, never thinking to incorporate it into breakfast. One weekend with friends, I decided to make a baked egg dish. I had an extra jar of pesto on hand, and in my experimental kitchen style, I threw a couple tablespoons into our skillet of eggs. The result was a win. Now, I love keeping a jar handy for all times of the day. This flavorful breakfast toast is warm, rich, satisfying, and utterly delicious.

1 slice good bread, I love sourdough for this one!

1 egg, soft boiled (see page 20)

1-2 Tbsp pesto, homemade or store-bought

2 Tbsp Parmesan

Seasoning of choice

Begin by toasting your bread. I like to apply the pesto to the bread, then toast in the oven. You can also toast your bread in a toaster and add the pesto after. Once your bread is toasted, slice your soft boiled egg down the middle and place on the toast. Top with your shaved Parmesan and salt and pepper, or seasoning of your choice. For a bit of spice, a dash of cayenne is great on this toast.

TIP: Parmesan and pesto are notoriously good together. But if you don't have Parmesan, use a different sharp cheese. Manchego or sharp cheddar are both great options.

Makes 1 slice

SMOKED SALMON + AVOCADO + CUCUMBER + SPROUTS

For mornings on the go, it is often easy to forget to give our bodies the fuel they need to operate efficiently throughout the day. Smoked salmon is something I like to keep stocked because of its protein content and Omega-3 benefits. It's packed with great nutrients to sustain a packed schedule. Plus, these cucumber ribbons make for such a beautiful presentation. So whether you're taking a moment to fill your body with nourishment in the morning, or you're hosting a brunch and need a lovely presentation, this toast is fantastic, life-giving fuel.

2 slices good bread, I'm using sourdough

2 oz quality smoked salmon

2 Tbsp cream cheese

1 Persian cucumber

¼ avocado

1 handful sprouts

Watercress, optional

Olive oil

Salt + pepper

Toast the bread using your method of choice. While your bread is toasting, use a vegetable peeler to "ribbon" your cucumbers. Lay the cucumber flat on a cutting board and thinly run the blade of the peeler down the length of the cucumber. You can also use a mandolin! Slice your avocado into thin slices and drizzle with a bit of citrus. When your bread is toasted, spread each slice with 1 tablespoon cream cheese. Then, assemble your toasts! Begin with the smoked salmon, then top with cucumber ribbons, avocado, sprouts, and watercress, or any other additional greens. Drizzle with olive oil, and season with salt and pepper.

TIP: If you don't like the flavor of smoked salmon, this toast is also good with pan fried tofu, or your protein of choice!

Makes 2 slices

AVOCADO + BACON + A FRIED EGG

This is perhaps one of the most simple and delicious go-to breakfast toasts of all time. For nearly two years I worked with my dear friend Courtney in Los Angeles. Each day, we'd begin by having breakfast together. This recipe became a staple of ours. Efficient and delicious, this toast is all about the breakfast basics. Packed with healthy fats, protein, and loads of flavor, this meal can sustain you through any kind of morning.

1 slice good bread

½ medium avocado

1 cage-free egg

2 slices bacon, you can also use turkey bacon, or omit

1 tsp good seasoning, I'm using a sesame + poppy seed blend (see page 21)

Olive oil

Begin by cooking the bacon. Pan fry at medium heat until crispy, or bake at 400° on a baking sheet for about 15 minutes. Set the cooked bacon aside on a paper towel to absorb extra grease. Slice your avocado thinly. Scoop out the slices and drizzle with lemon juice or another citrus to keep it from going brown. While toasting your bread, fry your egg in a pan with a dash of olive oil (see page 20 for instructions). I like my egg over easy, but you can cook as you prefer. Then, assemble! Top your toast evenly with the avocado, bacon slices, and fried egg. Drizzle the whole toast with olive oil, then add your favorite seasoning.

TIP: If you're hosting a group for breakfast, you can make a whole pan of these at one time! Toast your bread with olive oil on a baking sheet while cooking a whole pan of bacon in the oven at the same time.

Makes 1 slice

BERRY + ALMOND + ROSEMARY + WHIPPED CREAM CHEESE

While I was in college, our dining hall had a fantastic salad bar. It was there I discovered and got hooked on honey roasted almonds. I put them in and on everything. When I began cooking for myself later on, I started buying them in bulk, and they are now always stocked in my pantry. They add a delicious, nutty, sweet crunch to salads, smoothies, desserts, and even toasts! This toast has that amazing honey-nut crunch, coupled with fresh rosemary. It's an easy one to nibble on, set aside, and come back to. Sometimes I'll double this recipe in the morning and warm up the other toast later in the day.

---

1 large slice good bread

6 raspberries

2 large strawberries

8 blueberries

1 Tbsp pomegranate seeds

2 Tbsp whipped cream cheese

1 Tbsp honey roasted almonds

1 sprig rosemary

Honey for drizzle, optional

Toast your slice of bread. When your toast is golden, spread it with the whipped cream cheese. Top with all of the berries, then sprinkle with almonds, pomegranate seeds, and rosemary sprigs. For a little extra sweetness, drizzle with honey!

TIP: You can buy whipped cream cheese, or you can whip it yourself! Let the cream cheese come to room temperature, then beat it in a mixer. Slowly add 1-2 tablespoons milk until it reaches your desired consistency!

Makes 1 slice

SAUTÉED SPINACH + GARLIC
+ A POACHED EGG

I used to be highly intimidated to poach eggs. It's quite a challenge and can go very wrong. But, that is some of the fun in the kitchen; trying and trying again. After watching many YouTube videos and failing quite a few times, I finally got the hang of poaching. It's now one of my favorite ways to eat eggs. If you've never poached an egg before, give it a try! And don't fret if it doesn't work perfectly the first time. Maybe you'll even be a kitchen wizard who masters it on the first try! Regardless, there is always power in attempting to do the things that intimidate us. I've nicknamed this toast The Popeye because it's loaded with sautéed spinach. It is a great way to get the greens and protein you need all in one toast.

1 slice good bread

1 egg, poached (see page 20)

1 Tbsp olive or avocado oil

3 cups spinach

2 garlic cloves

1 tsp seasoning of your choice

In a skillet or frying pan, heat your oil. Peel and chop your garlic cloves and add to the hot oil, stirring for about 1 minute. Add in your spinach and cook until it's wilted and cooked through. Set aside. Boil a small pot of water and poach that egg! While your egg is poaching, pop the bread in a toaster. Remove the toast, then top with the spinach and garlic mixture. Drain all the water from your poached egg, then add it on top of the spinach. Top with salt, pepper, or your seasoning of choice!

TIP: This toast is great with a variety of greens. You can use kale, Swiss chard, or any other of your choice! Craving a little spice on there? Try adding Sriracha or hot sauce for an extra wake-me-up kick.

Makes 1 slice

MANGO + COCONUT BUTTER + PECAN + FLAXSEED

I love both really indulgent and really healthy things. Often in cooking, I like to eat a bit of both, and this toast is just that. The creamy flavors of ricotta and mango match perfectly with the crunchy, buttery notes of the pecans and flax. Flaxseed is known to be one of nature's most powerful foods. It is rich in Omega-3s, both insoluble and soluble fiber, and contains lignans, which have plant estrogen and antioxidant qualities. So even in the indulgence of this toast, you are still getting a meal full of health benefits.

2 slices good bread, this is great with ciabatta!

½ ripe mango, thinly sliced

2-3 Tbsp coconut butter

¼ cup pecans

2 Tbsp flaxseed

Honey, optional

Sea salt

Begin by toasting your bread. When your toast is golden, spread each slice with equal amounts of coconut butter. Load your toast with mango slices. Crush the pecans in your hand and sprinkle evenly. Lastly, top with flaxseed! If you're craving a bit more sweetness, drizzle the toasts with honey or agave. Sprinkle with a finishing dash of sea salt.

TIP: I love tropical flavors with flax, so pineapple is another great option for this toast. If you don't have (or don't like) coconut butter, you can also use the solids from coconut milk. Refrigerate a can of coconut milk overnight, then use the solid part of the milk as your spread.

Makes 2 slices

SMASHED ENGLISH PEA + A SOFT BOILED EGG

There are some cities in the world that make our spirits come a bit more alive. London is that city for me. I feel connected and so inspired each time I visit. Over the past six years, I've had the opportunity to spend quite a bit of time in this magical place, and have watched the food scene grow into a delicious, thriving culture. Chefs are coming from all over the world to rival their restaurants in this busy global center. One thing the English do really well? Peas and toast. Yup, you heard me, peas. This toast is loaded with smashed English peas (or mash) and a perfectly done soft boiled egg. Even if peas aren't your jam, give it try.

2 slices good bread, I'm using sourdough

2 eggs, soft boiled (see page 20)

½ cup English peas

1 Tbsp olive oil

Seasoning of choice

In a small saucepan, add your peas with ¼ cup water and bring to a simmer over medium heat. Allow the peas to cook for 6-8 minutes, or until they're tender. Remove from the heat and drain. Toast your bread however you prefer. Once the peas have cooled a bit, add the olive oil and smash them using your hands or a masher. Top each toast with ¼ cup of the pea mixture. Peel your soft boiled eggs, then slice and arrange one egg on each toast. Sprinkle with salt, pepper, or any seasoning you like!

TIP: If you get the chance to go to London, make sure to check out The Breakfast Club. Or, if you hit up any English pub, be sure to order the full English breakkie with beans and tomato. It's delightful.

Makes 2 slices

SAVORY

These are the salty, satisfying toasts! The ones that offer a little more substance and heartiness. These savory treats can be eaten any time, but I love to make one for a mid-day lunch break. The nature of toasts is quite casual, making them a great tool to invite a friend over for lunch, or even hand off an extra slice at your workplace.

Offering someone toast is an approachable way to welcome friendship. And truly, healthy and wise friends are life's greatest gifts. They remind us who we are and help push us into the best version of ourselves. Who we surround ourselves can give us so much life, or in the wrong hands, can take it away.

This chapter is full of vibrant veggies, greens, and proteins to offer you some quick (and healthy) meal ideas. Most can be made in just a few steps, and will leave you feeling nourished and content. My hope is that these savory toasts allow you to invite someone (or many someones!) in for shared space and good conversation.

AVOCADO + DRIED FIG + GORGONZOLA

Figs and gorgonzola! They're such a beautiful match. I like to imagine them as a married couple that offers a perfect balance to one another. The gorgonzola is intense, outgoing, and bold; while the fig is soft, sweet, and tender. Together, they're a brilliant combo. In all relationships, it's an amazing thing to be surrounded by people who are gifted in ways that balance us. When we pursue relationships that both challenge and complement us, we grow and become better versions of ourselves. This toast is always a reminder to me that we aren't meant to stand alone, and often, the most magical flavors of ourselves are discovered alongside other people.

2 slices good bread, I'm using rye

½ avocado

½ lime or lemon

2 Tbsp crumbled gorgonzola

4-6 dried figs, chopped into bite-size pieces

Olive oil to drizzle

Begin by toasting your bread. When your bread is toasted, smash ¼ avocado onto each slice. Squeeze lime or lemon juice all over the avocado. Top with your crumbled gorgonzola and dried figs. Drizzle your toasts with olive oil to finish.

TIP: This toast is just as delicious with fresh figs! If figs are in season, try subbing out the dried fruit for the fresh version. It creates an equally yummy flavor!

Makes 2 slices

BBQ LIME SHRIMP

I so enjoy when an experiment in the kitchen creates a new favorite recipe. This toast is one of those unintentional finds. My good friend Jonny makes an unbelievably mouth watering BBQ sauce that is so darn good. While visiting in Madison, I could not stop eating it. Throughout my visit, I found myself repeatedly sneaking into the refrigerator to look for vehicles to down this delicious sauce on. Finally, I decided it just needed to make its way onto toast. With some citrusy shrimp, loads of BBQ sauce, and lime zest, this toast tastes like a backyard summer barbecue.

4 slices good bread

2 Tbsp cream cheese

¼ cup of your favorite BBQ sauce

12-16 cooked shrimp

2 limes

Olive oil

Preheat your oven to 400˚. Place your bread on a baking sheet. Spread each slice of bread with ½ tablespoon cream cheese. Then, top with 1 tablespoon BBQ sauce. Place 3-4 cooked shrimp on each slice, then drizzle lightly with olive oil. Squeeze the lime juice all over the toasts. Bake for about 8 minutes, or until the bread is toasty. Remove from the oven, and using a microplane, cover each toast with a healthy amount of zest. Serve warm!

TIP: To make eating these a bit simpler, remove the tails of your shrimp beforehand!

Makes 4 slices

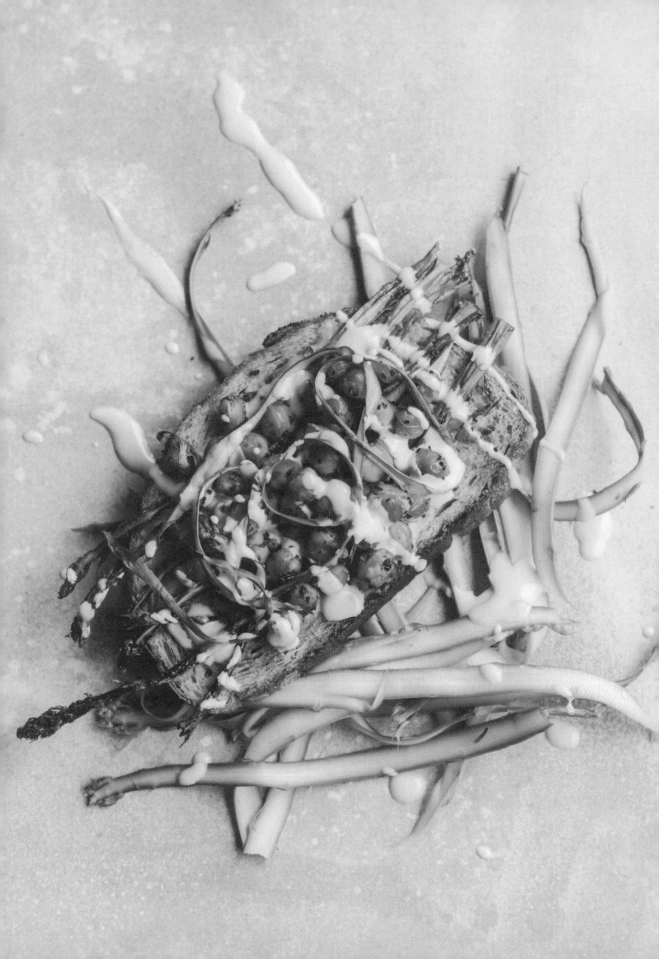

ASPARAGUS + GARBANZO + TAHINI

My sister-in-law Danielle comes from the most lovely Lebanese family. When she married my brother, I was introduced to her Aunt May, a vivacious, loving, and warm woman who loves to cook for people. She introduced me to authentic Lebanese food, full of garlic, lemon, and the most delicious Mediterranean flavors. Often times, she'll use my favorite, tahini. Anytime I'm craving a salty snack with a creamy sauce, I use tahini. It is so tasty, yet neutral enough that it can complement so many other flavors. I love a very liberal drizzle of tahini on each of these toasts, and sometimes make a bit extra for the joys of dipping.

2 slices good bread

8 large asparagus spears, sliced in half, lengthwise

¼ cup garbanzo beans

1 Tbsp tahini

½ tsp sea salt

½ tsp garlic powder

Olive oil

Preheat the oven to 400°. Slice your asparagus in half and place on a baking sheet. Drizzle with a dash of olive oil and roast for 12 minutes. Remove from the oven. Whisk your tahini with 1-2 teaspoons water, sea salt, and garlic powder. On each slice of bread, arrange your roasted asparagus and garbanzo beans evenly. Drizzle each toast with a bit of tahini sauce, setting aside about 1 tablespoon for after baking. Dash each toast with salt and pepper. Place your assembled toasts on a baking sheet, and bake for 8-10 minutes, or until golden. Remove from oven and drizzle with remaining tahini sauce.

TIP: If you happen to have access to a Mediterranean grocery store, grab a jar of zaatar spice to really enhance the flavors of this toast!

Makes 2 slices

HUMMUS + ROASTED PEPPER + PROSCIUTTO

In the kitchen, I like to use shortcuts when they're worth it. A good shortcut can alleviate any unnecessary stress in cooking. While there are times that I love making my own pizza dough, or spending hours chopping and roasting veggies, I always suggest using the worthy alternatives. For example, this toast calls for roasted peppers and hummus. You could absolutely roast your own peppers and make homemade hummus. But, there are some fantastic store bought options that allow this toast to be a 3 minute assembly, making the shortcuts completely worth it for an easy, delicious meal.

2 slices good bread

2 Tbsp hummus

½ cup roasted red peppers

2 slices prosciutto

½ Tbsp olive oil

Some greens

Sea salt + pepper

Begin by toasting your bread. Spread your toasts evenly with the hummus. Layer on your roasted red peppers. Top with prosciutto, curling the slices to fit on the toast. If you prefer to eat them warm, you can pop the assembled toasts in the oven for a few minutes on a baking sheet. Garnish with greens, olive oil, salt, and pepper!

TIP: This toast is complemented so well by a spicy hummus! I love to use a cilantro jalapeño hummus, or even a Sriracha hummus.

Makes 2 slices

SMASHED SWEET POTATO + RADISH
+ PARSLEY + PARMESAN

Playing with color is so fun, isn't it? When I was a little girl I would get ecstatic about a new coloring book and a box of crayons. I loved reading the names of each color and arranging the box in a way where they complemented one another. Food has become like that for me. Gathering a variety of colorful ingredients to play with brings me so much freedom and youthfulness. Keeping it childlike in the kitchen seems to dissipate the fear of failing, and it empowers creativity. I love the vibrant pinks, oranges, and greens of this toast. It's a masterpiece of color and a bright way to indulge in a meal.

4 slices good bread

1 large sweet potato, cooked

2 radishes

2 Tbsp shaved Parmesan

2 Tbsp parsley, chopped finely

Lemon juice + olive oil, optional

Begin by toasting your slices of bread. Scoop out the inside of your cooked sweet potato, and smash evenly onto each toast. Thinly slice your radish, then arrange on top of the smashed sweet potato. Top with shaved Parmesan, parsley, lemon juice, and olive oil.

TIP: If you don't have a sweet potato on hand, roasted squash is a great substitution for this toast! Additionally, if you don't have parsley, you could use cilantro, chives, or basil as an alternative.

Makes 4 slices

YELLOW ASPARAGUS + BROCCOLINI
+ PARMESAN

A great way to elevate your toast game is to proactively think of what you have on hand that can go on bread. When I have leftovers from dinner, I like to imagine how they could work on toast the next day. This way of thinking ahead allows for a little more creativity and a lot less waste in the kitchen. The origin of this toast came from leftover roasted veggies that were so good I didn't want to throw them out. With a little bit of imagination, crafting toasts can teach you how to play with flavor and resourcefully use what you already have! For a quick veggie-packed dinner, use this toast as a go-to.

---

4 slices good bread

8 large spears yellow asparagus, halved lengthwise

4 large stalks broccolini

¼ cup shaved Parmesan

2 Tbsp olive oil, divided

Salt + pepper

Preheat your oven to 425˚. On a baking sheet, toss the yellow asparagus and broccolini with 1 tablespoon olive oil and a dash of salt. Pop in the oven and bake for 15 minutes, or until the asparagus begins to golden (if you have leftover roasted vegetables, omit this step!). Remove from the oven and place the veggies on a plate.

Arrange your bread on the same baking sheet. Place the cooked veggies on each toast evenly across the width of the bread. Place the pan back in the oven and bake for 8 minutes, or until the bread begins to crisp around the edges. Remove from the oven and sprinkle each toast with 1 tablespoon Parmesan. Drizzle lightly with the remaining olive oil, and season with salt and pepper.

TIP: This toast is great with any roasted vegetable. For an added kick, add some chopped garlic or onion while roasting!

Makes 4 slices

LENTIL + CHERRY TOMATO + WHIPPED FETA

I have quite a few friends who no longer eat meat. When they come over for dinner, I love making sure I can still create a meal that is tasty and fully satisfying. Enter lentils. They're an incredible legume packed with protein and fiber, and have been in the human diet for thousands of years. They're great for digestive health and are known to stabilize blood sugar. Plus, the lentil is so versatile. It can stand alone or be added to a variety of dishes. Their taste is quite neutral, able to take on the flavor of their surrounding ingredients. This toast pairs lentils with strong flavors of tomato and feta to create a hearty, healthy meal.

2 slices good bread

2 Tbsp whipped feta (see page 21)

¼ cup cooked lentils, you can purchase pre-cooked

¼ cup cherry tomatoes

Seasoning of choice

Begin by toasting your bread. In a small sauce pan, warm your lentils on medium heat with a dash of olive oil, stirring occasionally until warmed through (about 3 minutes). Spread each toast with 1 tablespoon whipped feta. Pile the warm lentils evenly over the feta. Arrange the cherry tomatoes on top, then sprinkle your toasts with your favorite seasoning.

TIP: If you're looking to avoid dairy, I've enjoyed substituting a vegan cream cheese here. Hummus also works as a great base!

Makes 2 slices

APPLE + GOUDA + THYME

Cheese and apples? Yes please. During my time in London, we spent so much time having "picky bits" at the park. We'd load up on bites and snacks, grab a great bottle of wine, and linger over them. Picky bits are essentially just that: bits, or bites, of apples, nuts, fruits, and various cheeses that you pick at. Sometimes we'd fancy it up with various charcuterie and jam, but fruit and cheese was our staple. This toast is inspired by my love of these meals. With the simplicity of apples and cheese, and strong, fragrant flavors of gouda and thyme, this toast is a great fix for a savory craving.

4 slices good bread, I like to use a grainy baguette

1 large apple, I'm using a honey crisp!

2-3 oz quality gouda

1 Tbsp fresh thyme

Olive oil + honey to drizzle

Sea salt

Begin by toasting your bread. Core your apple, then slice thinly. Once your bread is toasty, layer each piece with an apple slice and a thin slice of Gouda, repeating the process across the whole toast. Drizzle each with a bit of olive oil, honey, and sea salt. Lastly, top with your thyme!

TIP: I love creating a toast bar with apples and cheese! It's perfect for entertaining. On a large cheese board or cutting board, arrange an assortment of toasts, cheeses, and fruits. Apples, berries, plums, and peaches all go great with cheese. Then, add little bowls of flavored honey, jams, and greenery to jazz up the platter!

Makes 4 slices

THE CAPRESE

Traveling has always been a priority to me. I tend to be quite the adventurer and love the way that visiting different cultures stretches us. The newness and discomfort it brings are foundational to interpersonal growth. When we are curious and open minded, new people and places can shift how we think, what we hunger for, and add depth to our human experience. In my early 20s, I was able to spend some time in Italy and discovered the classic caprese salad: a layering of fresh mozzarella, basil, and tomato. Along with slow eating, great wine, and celebration around food, the caprese is a staple I've happily adopted from Italian culture.

2 slices good bread, I love a rustic, crusty bread for this!

1 large tomato, sliced

3-4 oz fresh mozzarella, sliced into ¼ inch slices

6-8 large basil leaves

2 Tbsp pesto

Salt, pepper, and olive oil

Begin by toasting your bread. Slice your tomato and mozzarella. Layer your toast, alternating the mozzarella, tomato, and basil leaves. Repeat until you reach the end of your slice. Top each toast with 1 tablespoon pesto. Drizzle with olive oil, salt, and pepper to finish!

TIP: Try mixing up The Caprese with heirloom tomatoes to add some variation in color and flavor. Or, if you're a burrata lover like I am, try substituting it in for the mozzarella!

Makes 2 slices

SPICED GARBANZO + WHIPPED FETA
+ CILANTRO + TAHINI

Health is a loaded conversation. It is often difficult to know what truly is healthy. In my own food journey, I've loved learning how to listen to my body. It's much easier said than done, but paying attention to how your body reacts, feels, and responds to certain foods is key. While I love a good burger from time to time, I also love quality vegetarian recipes that offer me a protein packed, sustaining meal. I began making this toast on days I was craving a full, robust meal, but wanted to avoid meat. The spice of the garbanzos and rich flavors of feta and cilantro match wonderfully together. Adding on tahini is the perfect final touch!

2 large slices good bread

3 Tbsp whipped feta

½ cup garbanzo beans

½ Tbsp olive oil

1 Tbsp herbes de Provence

1 Tbsp tahini

2 tsp warm water

½ tsp sea salt

2 Tbsp chopped cilantro

Salt + pepper

In a small saucepan, add your garbanzo beans, herbes de Provence, a dash of salt, and olive oil. Cook on medium heat for 4-5 minutes, or until heated through. Remove from heat. In a small bowl, whisk your tahini, warm water, and sea salt. Set aside. Toast your slices of bread. Spread each slice evenly with the whipped feta (see page 21 for instructions). Top each with half of the herbed garbanzo beans. Finish the toasts by topping with cilantro and an even drizzle of the tahini. Add salt and pepper to taste.

TIP: Garbanzos are a fantastic bean, but other beans can be replaced for the same richness. Try white beans or even pinto beans instead!

Makes 2 slices

SWEET POTATO PURÉE + WHIPPED FETA + MICROGREENS

Have you experimented with purées? I love them! They're a fun way to take a basic food and elevate the consistency and flavor. You can make vegetable purées, legume purées, and even fruit purées. They make great toppings for many dishes, and create a wonderful base for toasts. The sweet potato purée used on this toast is delightful. I often make a batch to use as a dip for a charcuterie board, or even as a throw-in for quinoa and pasta.

1 thick slice good, grainy bread

2 Tbsp sweet potato purée

2 Tbsp whipped feta (see page 21)

1 Tbsp microgreens

Olive oil

Salt + pepper

To make the sweet potato purée, blend one cooked sweet potato (with skin removed) in a food processor with ½ tablespoon olive oil until completely whipped and blended. Toast your slice of bread. Spread 2-3 tablespoons sweet potato purée onto the toast. Add 2 tablespoons whipped feta onto the purée, spreading evenly. Top your toast with microgreens, salt, and pepper. Drizzle the whole toast with a bit of olive oil to finish!

TIP: These are a great Thanksgiving toast! You can make an entire batch on a baking sheet, and serve as a fantastic appetizer for your feast.

Makes 1 slice

CREAM CHEESE + HEIRLOOM
+ RED ONION + CHIVE

Simplicity often wins in my kitchen. While I do enjoy a long cooking process, sometimes it's nice to just keep it easy. I never want cooking to feel like a chore, so on days where I need some quick nourishment but still want to eat something delicious, I remind myself it doesn't have to take long to make something wonderful. This toast is loaded with color and only takes a few moments to assemble, so you can grab some sustenance and get on with the day.

2 slices good bread, I'm using rye

2 Tbsp cream cheese

½ cup miniature heirloom tomatoes

¼ red onion, thinly sliced

2 Tbsp fresh chopped chives

Sea salt + pepper

Slice or chop your heirloom tomatoes. In a small bowl, toss them with a dash of sea salt and pepper. Toast your slices of bread. Spread each toast with 1 tablespoon cream cheese. Arrange the tomatoes on top of the cream cheese, then top with the red onion and chopped chives.

TIP: To thinly slice a red onion, cut off each end, then slice in half. Peel the skin off the onion. Lay one half flat on the counter, and slice radially towards the center of the onion!

Makes 2 slices

HUMMUS + FETA + CHARRED CORN + WATERCRESS

When I moved to LA, I knew that I needed a good community to survive in this city. My friends here have truly become family; giving me a sense of belonging, purpose, and identity. We recently began monthly family dinners - an evening filled with endless amounts of food, delicious wine, and intentional conversations. They're a space to grow deeper in relationship, experience a sense of family, and laugh. I often end up cheffing these evenings, and during the summer months I've loved to create menus that incorporate the season. With its fresh, charred corn, this toast creates an experience of outdoor dining. Topped with loads of hummus, feta, and greens, it's the perfect appetizer toast for any family gathering.

8 slices good bread, a baguette is great for appetizer size

½ cup hummus

½ cup crumbled feta

2 ears fresh corn, or 1-2 cups canned or frozen corn

1 cup watercress

1 tsp cayenne

1 tsp cumin

Olive oil

Sea salt

Peel your corn and with a sharp knife, cut it by running the blade down the entire length of the ear. In a skillet, heat a bit of olive oil. Add your corn, cayenne, and cumin and cook on medium-high heat, or until your corn begins to blister. Remove from heat and set aside. Toast your bread. Spread each slice with a spoonful of hummus, and top with the charred corn. Then, add the crumbled feta and watercress. Drizzle each toast with olive oil, and top with a dash salt.

TIP: The next time you dine with family or host a dinner party, try asking an intentional table question. It's a great way to dive deeper into friendship and learn more about the people you love.

Makes 8 slices

BLUE CHEESE + MANGO + CRISPY PROSCIUTTO

I first learned about crispy prosciutto one evening while making a salad that called for bacon. I didn't have any, and had no desire to go to the grocery store, but knew the salad just needed something with that salty and crispy kick. So, I looked in my refrigerator and found a few slices of prosciutto. I popped them on a baking sheet and cooked them through. The result was magnificent! Crispy prosciutto has the same salty bite as bacon, but is just a bit thinner with a slightly different flavor. This toast has a beautiful intensity with the sharpness of blue cheese, sweet notes of mango, and perfect, salty crunch to top it off.

1 slice good bread

¼ mango, cut into thin slices

1 Tbsp crumbled blue cheese

1-2 slices prosciutto

Olive oil

To make crispy prosciutto, lay the prosciutto flat on a baking sheet and bake at 400° until it resembles a dark, crispy color similar to bacon (about 10 minutes). While the prosciutto crisps, toast your bread. Then, top your bread with crumbled blue cheese. Arrange your sliced mango on top of the cheese. Remove the prosciutto from the oven and crumble over your toast. If you like, you can pop the assembled toast back in the oven for 2-3 minutes to warm through and melt the blue cheese a bit.

TIP: If you're not a fan of stinky cheeses, you can go with one that is more mild. A goat cheese or a stilton would also work great on this toast!

Makes 1 slice

ROASTED CARROT + PESTO + PISTACHIO

When I photographed Toast with Paper Antler, we had the best time taste-testing all 62 creations. We invited neighbors and friends over for a Toast party, with loads of food and some delicious tequila cocktails. As I encouraged Michelle to try this one, she was hesitant. Not much of a pesto or carrot fan, she was going to pass, but ended up sneaking one bite. To her surprise, it turned out to be her favorite of all the recipes. The combination of sweetness from the carrot and saltiness from the pesto work so well together. Plus, carrots are known to enhance skin health, slow aging, and help cleanse the body. Flavor-packed and loaded with health benefits? What's not to love?

4 slices good bread

12-16 mini tri-colored carrots, sliced in half lengthwise

1 Tbsp olive oil

1 tsp sea salt

2 garlic cloves, chopped finely

¼ cup pesto (see page 21 to make your own)

2 Tbsp pistachios

Preheat your oven to 425˚. On a baking sheet, toss your carrots, chopped garlic, olive oil, and sea salt. Roast in the oven and bake for 25-30 minutes, or until the carrots are tender and begin to char. Remove carrots from the oven and set onto a plate or dish.

Arrange your bread on the same baking sheet. Top each slice with 1 tablespoon pesto. Arrange the roasted carrots on top of the toasts, and sprinkle with pistachios. Then, drizzle lightly with olive oil. Place the baking sheet back in the oven for about 8 minutes, or until edges of your toasts begin to brown. Serve warm, with extra pesto on the side.

TIP: These carrots are SO good roasted on their own. Make a double batch for dinner one night, then save the remainder to make toasts with the next day.

Makes 4 slices

BUTTERNUT SQUASH + GORGONZOLA + ARUGULA

During squash season, some hoarding tendencies come out in me. I love all kinds of squash. I'll even buy 10 at a time, then bake multiples in my oven so that they're cooked and on hand for any kind of recipe. Squash can be added to salads, pastas, sandwiches, omelets, and of course, toasts. You can keep a cooked squash in your refrigerator for up to a week, and pull it out anytime to enhance a dish or just eat solo! This toast is a two minute make, and is full of delicious, comforting flavors.

1 slice good bread

2-3 Tbsp cooked butternut squash

1-2 Tbsp gorgonzola cheese

1 small handful arugula

Salt + pepper

Olive oil, optional

Toast your bread. Scoop out your cooked squash and arrange on top of the toast. If the squash is not yet cooked, you can pop the whole thing in the oven at 425° for an hour, or until cooked through. Top the squash with gorgonzola and arugula. For extra flavor, drizzle with olive oil and dash with salt and pepper!

TIP: Looking for a little crunch? This toast goes so well with sunflower seeds, a bit of flax or hemp seed, or any nut of your choice!

Makes 1 slice

AVOCADO + CRISPY KALE + TAHINI + SEASONING SALT

One of my favorite things about living in California is the abundance of avocados. Growing up in my hometown in Michigan, avocados were a rarity. Now, I feel spoiled with them! When I have a craving for avocado, I head over to my friend Sarah's backyard to raid her avocado tree that boasts thousands of the fruit each year. It's amazing. This recipe is a simple upgrade to your standard avocado toast. The crisp of the kale and the richness of the avocado create a delightfully filling, healthy meal.

1 large slice good bread, I'm using a seedy grain bread from a local baker

1 cup chopped kale

1-2 Tbsp olive oil

½ avocado

1 Tbsp tahini

Sea salt + pepper

Seasoning of your choice

Begin by crisping your kale. This can be done in a cast iron skillet on high heat with a bit of olive oil and salt. Sauté the kale until it begins to brown. Alternatively, you can crisp the kale in the oven at 450° for 12-15 minutes with olive oil and salt.

Whisk your tahini with a dash of sea salt and 1-2 teaspoons water until it becomes a drizzling consistency. Next, toast your bread. Pile your toast high with crispy kale. Remove the pit from your avocado, slice thinly, remove with a spoon, and place on top of the kale. Drizzle the toast with your tahini sauce and top with extra seasoning, sea salt, and pepper!

TIP: You can also crisp your kale in a toaster oven! Spritz your kale leaves with a few sprays of olive or coconut oil and toast for 6-8 minutes, or until golden.

Makes 1 slice

ACORN SQUASH + PISTACHIO + BROCCOLINI + SEASONING

Pistachios are such a delicious nut. I have fond childhood memories of my dad cracking pistachios open while watching Dan Rather on summer evenings. They're full of body and crunch, and are a delightful addition to toasts. Quite neutral, they play an excellent flavor-building role. With some cooked squash and broccolini, this toast is full of warm fall flavors and makes for a perfectly healthy, comforting meal on a cool evening.

2 slices good bread

½ - ¾ cup cooked acorn squash (see page 17 for substitutions ideas)

1-2 Tbsp olive oil

2 Tbsp shelled pistachios

4-6 sprigs broccolini

Seasoning of your choice

Begin by roasting the broccolini. Preheat the oven to 450˚. Place the broccolini on a baking sheet and drizzle with olive oil and sea salt. Bake for 10-12 minutes.

Place ¼ cup squash on each slice of bread, then smash it lightly using a fork. Remove your broccolini from the oven and reduce the oven temperature to 400˚. Arrange the broccolini on top of the smashed squash. Place each toast on your same baking sheet. Drizzle with olive oil and sprinkle each piece with 1 tablespoon pistachios. Top with seasoning, and place in the oven for 8-10 minutes, or until the toasts are golden.

TIP: Squash is full of antioxidants and a great base for any toast! You can mix up the type of squash you use to try different flavor variations.

WHIPPED FETA + HEIRLOOM + BASIL + PESTO

Your demeanor sets the entire tone for anyone entering your kitchen. When I'm asked about the art of hosting, this is the first piece of advice that pops in my head. The presence of the host - their attitude, stress levels, and energy - creates the experience around a meal for guests. I strongly believe in the power of hosting yourself first, because it is ultimately the way you will host others. Though it's simple, taking care of yourself is key! I like to sip on a glass of wine while cooking, and begin 30 minutes earlier than I think I need to. Whatever it may be, knowing what allows you to be the best version of yourself is the greatest gift you can give a guest. This toast is quick, lively, and an easy one to make in masses for any party you have.

4 slices good bread

1 cup miniature heirloom tomatoes, quartered

2 Tbsp pesto

1 cup fresh basil, divided and chopped

½ cup whipped feta (see page 21)

In a small bowl, mix your tomatoes, pesto, and half of your basil. Set aside. Toast your four slices of bread. Spread each slice with 2 tablespoons whipped feta. Evenly distribute the tomatoes on your toasts. Top with the remaining fresh basil!

TIP: If you're running short on time or don't have the necessary ingredients to make whipped feta, this toast works just fine with another variation of cheese. Choose one that is flavorful and salty to enhance the sweetness of the heirlooms.

Makes 4 slices

SUN-DRIED TOMATO + ROASTED TURKEY + CHEDDAR

I love Los Angeles with all of my heart. It's a city that inspires dreamers to fully chase what they long for. It has every culture, food, and ethnicity. When I moved to the West Coast, I found myself connecting to my dreams in a way that I didn't realize possible. I felt things come alive in me that I never knew existed. Relationships have had a significant impact on helping my dreams develop, but I love noticing the way that geography affects us as well. The flavors of this toast pull at my Midwest roots, but come together in a new form. In what ways do you feel connected to your location?

---

2 slices good bread

4 oz roasted turkey breast, thinly sliced

2 Tbsp sun-dried tomatoes

2 oz sharp cheddar, thinly sliced

Salt + pepper

Toast your bread. Top each toast with 2 ounces turkey breast, 1 tablespoon sun-dried tomatoes, and 1 ounce sharp cheddar. If you'd like to serve them warm, bake the toasts on a baking sheet at 350° for 10-12 minutes, or until the cheese is melted.

TIP: Roasted turkey can be swapped out for chicken, ham, or even roast beef. I like to use canned sun-dried tomatoes because they're packed in olive oil, bringing a bit more flavor to the toast.

Makes 2 slices

RICOTTA + CRISPY KALE + ROASTED SQUASH

Just like toast is a vehicle for a delicious and creative meal, food has always been the vehicle for my greatest love: hosting. Gathering friends and strangers around a table to share a meal allows space for people to be seen and known; something we can all benefit from a little more of in life. Discovering savory toasts has made the hosting game a bit less intimidating for me. This toast boasts warm flavors and a great salty crunch that is utterly satisfying. It's a fabulous hosting toast, only taking a few minutes to put together.

4 slices good bread

¼ butternut squash, cooked (about 1 ½ cups)

¼ cup ricotta

3 cups chopped kale

2 Tbsp olive oil, divided

Sea salt + pepper

Preheat your oven to 400˚. In a mixing bowl, using your hands, massage the kale with 1 tablespoon olive oil and ½ teaspoon sea salt. On a baking sheet, arrange your bread. Spread each slice with 1 tablespoon ricotta. Scoop spoonfuls of the cooked squash out of the peel, and evenly place on each toast. Top with kale. Drizzle all toasts with the remaining olive oil. Place the baking sheet on the top rack in your oven and bake for 10-12 minutes, or until your kale begins to crisp. You can even turn your broiler on for 1-2 minutes to allow the kale to fully crisp. Remove from the oven, season with salt and pepper, and serve warm!

TIP: Some grocery stores offer pre-cut butternut squash. If you don't have a whole roasted squash, you can roast some pre-cut squash in the oven at 400˚ for 20-25 minutes, or until golden and tender.

Makes 4 slices

HUMMUS + HEIRLOOM + ROSEMARY + BRIE

The French do cheese so well, don't they? In fact, they do food really well in general. They know the value of simplicity and slowness around food, and are fantastic at shopping locally. Their markets are loaded with freshly baked baguettes and endless varieties of cheese. This toast is inspired simply from my love of Brie. Named after the region in France where it originated, Brie has a creaminess that offers a bit of comfort in each bite. Along with a nice glass of red wine, this simple toast can be a delightful and comforting evening meal to wind down a long day.

1 large slice good bread

1 oz Brie, sliced

1-2 Tbsp hummus

½ cup sliced heirloom tomatoes

1 sprig fresh rosemary

Salt, pepper, and olive oil

Begin by toasting your bread. Then, spread evenly with hummus. Arrange your sliced Brie on top and layer with heirloom tomatoes. Sprinkle with small sprigs of fresh rosemary, then drizzle with olive oil, salt, and pepper to taste!

TIP: Don't think you like Brie? Try a few different kinds! Check out a local cheese market and ask to sample the varieties. Brie can vary in flavor, so you may be able to find one you enjoy!

Makes 1 slice

PROSCIUTTO + SHAVED ASPARAGUS + GOAT CHEESE

Charcuterie boards have become a staple at most events that I host. They are the centerpiece of a dinner or cocktail party, and can be loaded up with various dips, breads, cheeses, and always prosciutto. This beautifully sliced meat is lovely to create with because it takes on shape and adds a flavor kick to any dish. Learning to play with color and arrange a cheese and charcuterie board can be such a fun challenge. I often will do some inspiration research on Pinterest or Instagram to give myself a visual of what I'd like to create. This toast is a mini version of an eye-catching board. With the simple touch of shaved asparagus and well placed prosciutto, you'll end up with a beautiful, gourmet looking toast.

4 slices good bread

4-6 large asparagus spears

4 Tbsp goat cheese

4 slices quality prosciutto

Olive oil

Preheat your oven to 375°. Lay your sliced bread on a baking sheet and spread each slice with 1 tablespoon goat cheese. Arrange your prosciutto on each toast, twirling it with your hands to give it some dimension. Next, use a vegetable peeler to shave your asparagus. Run the peeler lengthwise along the asparagus spear to create thinly shaved ribbons. Top each toast with some asparagus ribbons, curling them for an extra touch of presentation. Drizzle the toasts with olive oil. Bake in the oven for 10-12 minutes, or until your prosciutto begins to crisp and your toast is golden.

TIP: To simplify shaving the asparagus, make sure you're using a sharp peeler. A quality peeler is key and makes shaving vegetables and fruits much easier when you've got the right tools.

Makes 4 slices

EGG SALAD + DILL

Our food preferences have always been profound to me. We all have opinions about what we do or don't like, but I love encouraging people to remain curious around their palette. This true curiosity allows us to be present. To enter into an experience without judgment of what is or should be, which is magical. I used to hate egg salad. I truthfully thought I'd never like it. At lunch one day, a friend ordered an egg salad sandwich and offered me a bite. Normally I would have refused, but a nudge of curiosity rose up in me. Not only did I realize my palette had changed, but it became a delicious, repeated toast for me. So, remain curious! The joy of food comes in the discovery of the unexpected.

4 slices good bread

4 eggs, hard boiled (see page 20)

2 Tbsp Greek yogurt

2 tsp Dijon mustard

½ lemon

½ cup dill, divided

Cayenne powder, or other seasoning of choice

Peel your hard boiled eggs and place them in a mixing bowl. Add the yogurt, mustard, lemon juice, and ¼ cup dill (chopped). Using a fork, mash all of the ingredients together to create an egg salad. Toast your slices of bread. Top each with ¼ of the egg salad mixture, then sprinkle with any seasonings you like and the remaining dill.

TIP: I like to triple the egg salad portion of this recipe to have some easy, protein packed goodness on hand!

Makes 4 slices

PULLED CHICKEN + LIME SLAW
+ THAI PEANUT SAUCE

Chicken on toast? It sounds strange, but trust... it is DELICIOUS. While grocery shopping, I often grab a rotisserie chicken and use it throughout my meals in the week. Even though I love cooking, it's a necessity to have a couple meals on hand that require little to no thought. Pulled chicken tacos, loaded chicken salads, or a plate of roasted chicken and sweet potatoes are some of the simple ways I like to keep meals healthy and efficient. This savory toast makes a complete meal from leftover ingredients for an entirely different (and easy!) lunch or dinner.

2 slices good bread

¼ cup cooked chicken, I'm using a rotisserie breast

1 Tbsp peanut butter

1 tsp soy sauce

1 tsp brown sugar

1 Tbsp hot water

¼ cup sliced cabbage

Juice of ½ lime

1 tsp garlic powder

1 Tbsp Greek yogurt

Cumin

Salt + pepper

Preheat your oven to 375˚. In a small bowl, whisk your peanut butter, soy sauce, brown sugar, and water until completely mixed (you can warm in the microwave to help this process). Set aside. In another small bowl, make your slaw by combining the cabbage, yogurt, lime juice, garlic powder, and a dash of salt.

Lay your sliced bread on a baking sheet. Spread each toast with the peanut sauce, reserving about half for topping. Load the toasts with shredded or chopped chicken. Next, add a bit of slaw to each, and finish by drizzling the remainder of your peanut sauce over the toasts. Bake for about 10 minutes, or until heated through. Sprinkle with a bit of cumin, salt, and pepper to finish.

TIP: Peanut sauce is a great addition to many foods! If you don't eat meat, this toast would be fantastic with tofu or even some seitan.

Makes 2 slices

SWEET POTATO + A HARD BOILED EGG + ROASTED GARLIC

I have notoriously low iron and am always looking for ways to up my intake. Sweet potatoes offer massive health benefits, and they happen to be a fantastic form of iron. They're also packed with Vitamin C which produces collagen and helps keep the skin youthful and glowy. Additionally, garlic is known to stabilize blood sugar levels, and eggs are packed with protein. With this toast you get a balanced, healthy meal full of nutrients and deliciousness.

2 slices good bread

1 egg, hard boiled (see page 20)

1 small sweet potato, cooked

3 garlic cloves, chopped

1 Tbsp olive oil

1 small handful greens

In a skillet, roast your garlic in olive oil over medium heat until fragrant and golden (about 3 minutes). Set aside. Toast your bread in the same skillet. Smash half of the cooked sweet potato (without the peel) onto each slice. Peel your hard boiled egg and cut into 6-8 slices. Top each toast with half of the egg slices. Evenly top with roasted garlic, season with sea salt and pepper, and sprinkle on some greens.

TIP: Roasted sweet potatoes are great to have on hand for many recipes. I like to buy a large bag, roast them for an hour at 400°, let them cool, and store in the refrigerator to grab later for a quick snack or to add to a dish.

Makes 2 slices

CRISPY KALE + PARMESAN + SESAME

Have you tried sesame oil? I'm obsessed! There is a large Korean market that I frequent here in Los Angeles, and I often stock up on this fragrant and robust oil. Used in dressings or to roast veggies, sesame oil offers a unique flavor to anything you're making. Sometimes in life we stick with what we know, and for a long time in my kitchen, my go-to was olive oil. While co-cheffing with a friend, I was introduced to sesame oil being used in a variety of dishes, and have since added it as the perfect punch to this simple, clean toast.

4 slices good bread

3 cups chopped kale

2 Tbsp sesame oil

¼ cup shaved Parmesan

1 Tbsp sesame seeds

1 Tbsp poppy seeds

Sea salt

Preheat your oven to 450°. In a large bowl, mix the kale with 1 tablespoon sesame oil and a dash of sea salt. Use your hands to fully coat the kale, massaging it for about 2 minutes. Bake the kale on a baking sheet for about 10 minutes, or until the edges begin to brown. While the kale is crisping, toast your bread (you can do this in the same oven!). Remove the kale from the oven and place a pile on each slice. Top your toasts with 1 tablespoon Parmesan each. Then, drizzle with the remaining sesame oil. Sprinkle with sesame seeds, poppy seeds, and a dash of salt.

TIP: If you have access to a local Asian supermarket, give it a visit! Some of the best sesame oils can be found there.

Makes 4 slices

SWEET

The way our bodies process food has always fascinated me. In our culture, we can have a hard time celebrating food. We're often taught that foods are either good or bad, and this language can create unnecessary anxiety, guilt, or emotion around something that is meant to be enjoyed.

Let's say you and I are going out to get cupcakes. If you are eating a cupcake to celebrate a job promotion, but I'm eating one to cope with a break-up, the very way we digest the cupcakes will be different. The stress in my body will create problems with my digestion. The cupcake, and the guilt about eating it, will actually leave me feeling worse. There is so much research on the connection between stress and weight gain. So often, it occurs because we haven't been taught to properly celebrate food!

Eating well is never about "should" or "should-not". It's about listening to your body, knowing the value of moderation, and practicing a life of balance. I hope these toasts inspire you to create a beautiful, sweet, celebratory treat to fully enjoy.

BLOOD ORANGE YOGURT + PEAR + ROSEMARY

I love to make (and eat) beautiful food. It matters. The process of nourishment begins with our eyes, and something profound happens when we take the time to intentionally give our bodies something beautiful. Creating beauty for ourselves and for others is something we are created for. We long for it, and in many ways, I think it can get us a little more free. True beauty is the ultimate form of inspiration. And the different colors and textures of food do just that: inspire. A meal can be a momentary form of art that shifts the entirety of a day. The colors of this toast inspire me, and together the flavors create an entirely beautiful experience. Dive in.

2 slices good bread

½ blood orange

¼ cup plain Greek yogurt

½ pear, thinly sliced

1 sprig rosemary

Honey, optional

Squeeze the juice of your blood orange into a small bowl. Add in the Greek yogurt and whisk to create the blood orange yogurt sauce. Toast your slices of bread. Add a dollop of yogurt sauce to each toast, then arrange the pear slices on top. Drizzle the remaining yogurt on the toasts and top with fresh rosemary sprigs. For some extra sweetness, drizzle on a bit of honey. Add pieces of peeled blood orange for more color and flavor!

TIP: If blood oranges aren't in season, a regular orange will work! You won't get that beautiful pink color, but the citrus taste will still be delicious.

Makes 2 slices

RASPBERRY + LEMON + RICOTTA + FLAX

This delicious toast is one that almost made it into the Sunrise chapter. Loaded with health benefits and fresh flavors, it could easily be served for breakfast. But with the rich, creamy ricotta and the vibrant lemon and raspberry, this toast reminds me of an indulgent bite of cheesecake. The lemon and berry combination is delightful and fragrant, and the crunch of the golden flax is divine. On an evening when I'm craving a sweet treat but still looking to keep it light, this toast is absolutely satisfying.

1 slice good bread

2 Tbsp fresh raspberries

1 heaping Tbsp ricotta

2 tsp golden flaxseed

2-3 tsp lemon zest

Toast your slice of bread. Top your toast with ricotta, spreading evenly. Arrange your raspberries across the toast. Sprinkle the flaxseed on top of the berries, then top with loads of lemon zest.

TIP: If you don't have or don't prefer flaxseed, you can also get great benefits and the same texture from hemp seed, cacao nibs, or even some chopped nuts!

Makes 1 slice

THE APPLE PIE

Craving that sweet, indulgent, nostalgic bite of apple pie? This toast is just the solution. It has all the flavors of homemade pie, but takes only a couple of minutes to make! I'm from a small Dutch town in Michigan, and over the holidays, my family does food well. We feast. And the largest part of our feast is always the dessert bar. We have endless options of pies, cakes, and of course, Midwest trifles. Coming from a Dutch family, apple pie is a must. I hope this toast reminds you of family traditions, and that you are filled with memories in each bite.

2 slices good bread

½ apple, thinly sliced

2 Tbsp fig jam or raw honey

2 Tbsp pecans and walnuts, mixed

1 tsp cinnamon

½ tsp nutmeg

½ tsp cloves

Honey, optional

Preheat your oven to 375˚. Place your two slices of bread on a baking sheet and spread each slice with 1 tablespoon fig jam or raw honey. Arrange your apple slices evenly among the toasts. Top with pecans and walnuts. Sprinkle with cinnamon, nutmeg, and cloves, and drizzle with extra honey (optional). Bake for 10-12 minutes, or until crusts begin to brown.

TIP: This toast works well with gluten-free bread! The spongy texture gives the toast a nice "crust-like" bite.

Makes 2 slices

BRIE + BERRY + WALNUT + PEAR

When I was 24, I got my first tattoo - "beloved". I had always really loved the word. It stuck out to me. A few years later, I made a journal and scripted the word on the cover. One afternoon while sitting at Starbucks, a man walked over, looked at my journal, and said "BE loved" to me. I was caught off guard, but his quick interaction got me thinking. Being loved is an action. It requires a posture of receiving. Beloved has become an anthem over my life. It represents response. It is about owning who we are, and allowing others to truly see us. This toast is one of a kind. It's a delight, full of unique flavors, and acts as a simple reminder of the individuality that each of us embodies.

---

2 slices good bread

3 strawberries

¼ pear

1 tsp honey

1 tsp butter

1 tsp cinnamon, divided

2 oz Brie, sliced

1 Tbsp Greek yogurt

Remove the stems from your strawberries, then slice. Chop your pear into bite size pieces. In a small sauce pan, melt the butter, honey, and ½ teaspoon cinnamon. Add your pears and strawberries to the mixture. Cook on low heat for 2-3 minutes, or until mixed and heated through. Remove mixture from the heat. Toast your bread. Next, top each toast with the sliced Brie. Then, using a spoon, dish out the pear and berry mixture. Lastly, top each toast with a dollop of Greek yogurt and a sprinkle of the remaining cinnamon.

TIP: Pear and strawberry are a fantastic combo, but any kind of berry has the ability to match with pear! Try subbing in raspberries or blackberries to switch up the flavor.

Makes 2 slices

APRICOT + WHIPPED CREAM CHEESE + HAZELNUT + HONEY

Adventure in the kitchen, and in life, is crucial. Once, my dear friend Lindsey and I signed up for a "pack your passport" trip. We weren't given any specifics, but loaded onto a bus with 40 strangers to go have an adventure. With full expectation to go international, we hilariously ended up in Las Vegas. Being positive types, we made it our own and loved it. Even though neither of us would have chosen Vegas as our destination, we knew if we fully entered into the experience it would be absolutely enjoyable. This toast is a bit of an adventurous one. I stumbled upon the flavor combination using leftover apricots and hazelnuts from a salad. By adding a good base and some honey, this experimental toast became an all-time favorite.

4 slices good bread

2 oz whipped cream cheese

¼ cup hazelnuts, lightly chopped

12 dried apricots

2-3 Tbsp honey

Toast your slices of bread. Evenly spread each piece of toast with ½ ounce whipped cream cheese. Using scissors or a sharp knife, cut your apricots into small pieces. Top each toast evenly with the apricots. Sprinkle with chopped hazelnuts and drizzle each toast with honey!

TIP: Be adventurous with this toast! If you don't have apricots, you can sub in other dried fruits like cranberries or dried cherries.

Makes 4 slices

BUTTER + SUGAR + CINNAMON

My best friend Michelle and I lived in downtown Chicago for a semester during college. We were in the heart of Uptown in a beautiful brownstone, living our best lives. Isn't it comical how hindsight offers endless clarity? We were babies at the time, but really thought of ourselves as grown adults. She and I were broke students who loved to procrastinate; making late-night snacks while staying up late finishing papers and talking about our current crushes. This toast became a nearly everyday affair. It's the ultimate simple comfort. I don't know if I'd choose to ever go back to my younger years, but I'm endlessly grateful for the ways they shaped me. Are there foods from your past that remind you of certain life seasons?

2 slices good sandwich bread

2 Tbsp butter

1 tsp cinnamon

2 Tbsp brown sugar

Dash of salt

Turn your oven to the broil setting. Spray a baking sheet with non-stick cooking spray. Then, place your two slices of bread on the baking sheet. Spread each slice of bread with 1 tablespoon butter. Sprinkle 1 tablespoon brown sugar evenly onto each toast, following with cinnamon and a dash of salt. Place the toasts under the broiler and watch carefully! They can cook very quickly, and are done with they're fully golden and bubbly.

TIP: If I don't have butter on hand, I really love the flavor of coconut oil on this toast! Try subbing it in for a different flavor experience.

Makes 2 slices

BLUEBERRY + BASIL + RICOTTA + PEPITAS

While growing up, my family would go to the blueberry fields each summer and spend a morning picking fresh Michigan blueberries. We'd then take them home and make endless jars of blueberry jam, blueberry pies, and delicious ice cream toppings. They're such an amazing fruit, and when they're in season, they rival any berry. The blueberries on this toast are perfectly paired with pepitas, a crunchy little seed found in certain varieties of pumpkins. It's a seemingly sweet toast with a delectable, crunchy ending.

1 slice good bread

2-3 Tbsp blueberries

1-2 Tbsp ricotta

1 Tbsp pepitas

1 basil leaf, chopped

Toast your slice of bread. Top the toast generously with ricotta. Add the blueberries and pepitas. Lastly, top with your chopped basil.

TIP: I love to toast my pepitas in the oven with a bit of olive oil and sea salt. It brings out their flavor and adds another simple touch to elevate your toast game.

Makes 1 slice

PEAR + WALNUT + GORGONZOLA + HONEY

I have recently begun to say I'm still a mystery to myself. Let me explain. My 20s were a decade of self work, with years of counseling and intention to be whole and well. Entering my 30s felt like a brand new level of freedom. I walked into a comfortability in my own skin that I didn't even know could exist. However, in all of our self-exploration, we are still mysteries with mountains of depth to discover. Just like our palettes change and develop, we as humans grow and evolve. I think this is life's most beautiful gift; the ability to change. Give yourself the freedom to try new things, maybe even a flavor you're not inclined to, and let yourself be surprised by what develops in you.

2 slices good bread

½ pear, thinly sliced

2 Tbsp raw honey

2 Tbsp chopped walnuts

2 Tbsp gorgonzola

Toast your slices of bread. Spread each toast with 1 tablespoon raw honey. Pile the slices of pear on top of the honey, then top with bits of gorgonzola and chopped walnuts.

TIP: Don't have raw honey? You can use regular. Or, try subbing in a jam for your base. Apricot, fig, or strawberry work great!

Makes 2 slices

NUTELLA + CARAMELIZED BANANA + GREEK YOGURT GLAZE

This toast is all about childlike wonder. I mean, is there anything more delicious than a spoonful of Nutella? It was the ultimate treat when I was younger. Even still, when I see a jar, my mouth begins to water. My friend Brittany used to make me caramelized bananas whenever I'd visit, and those crispy, sugary bananas became the inspiration for this toast. Because while regular bananas and Nutella are delicious together, caramelizing them brings this toast to a whole new level. With simple sandwich bread and a Greek yogurt glaze, I hope this toast stirs up all the wonders and joys of childhood in you!

2 slices good sandwich bread

1 banana, sliced

1 Tbsp butter

2 Tbsp Nutella

1 Tbsp Greek yogurt

½ Tbsp honey

In a small sauté pan, add your banana slices and butter. Cook on medium heat, stirring lightly to cook both sides of the banana slices. Continue to sauté until the slices are golden and caramelized on each side. Set aside. To make your yogurt glaze, whisk together the yogurt and honey in a small bowl. Add 1 teaspoon milk to thin the glaze if desired. Toast your bread. Spread each toast with 1 tablespoon Nutella. Spoon your caramelized bananas onto each toast. Drizzle with the yogurt glaze.

TIP: There are so many brands that now make chocolate-hazelnut spreads with less sugar and a higher nutritional content. If you're looking for a healthier option, try out Justin's Chocolate Hazelnut Butter, or even experiment with making your own! There are many recipes online.

Makes 2 slices

BLACKBERRY + ROSEMARY + GOAT CHEESE

I've always wanted a garden blooming with fresh rosemary and endless berries. In conversations with friends or while hosting a dinner party, I like to think about how our words can plant seeds into each other's emotional gardens. The words others say about our character can bring life to spaces that are yearning for definition and meaning. I often use the phrase, "calling out the gold". It's the concept that our words have power to call out identity, purpose, and life in someone. The very things we say we can orient someone's entire life. That is AMAZING! And such a heavy gift. Because within the same vain, our words can steal, wound, and plant weeds in someone's life. So plant seeds wisely! You carry more power than you know.

1 slice good bread

¼ cup blackberries

1 oz goat cheese

A few rosemary sprigs, chopped

Agave to drizzle, optional

Toast your slice of bread. Spread the goat cheese across your toast. Cut blackberries in half lengthwise, then top your toast with them. Add a few fresh sprigs of chopped rosemary. Drizzle with agave if you choose.

TIP: Mix it up and try adding a bit of balsamic glaze to this toast! It's delightful.

Makes 1 slice

WALNUT + GOAT CHEESE + FIG + HONEY

What does the word home mean to you? Now in my 30s, it evokes a range of emotion. There's a longing for my Midwest childhood, and an acute awareness of how Los Angeles, a city across the country, has become such a home to me. During one of my first visits to LA, I spent an evening at a friend's house in Pasadena. This toast was served as a party bite and each time I make it, I vividly think about that time of transition. I was terrified to leave the comfortable and move my entire life, yet also full of hope for the seasons ahead. Now, home seems to be a statement of belonging. Less so to a place, but more to people. With only a few ingredients and lots of flavor, this toast makes for a great staple in your home.

8 slices good bread, I suggest a baguette!

2 Tbsp chopped walnuts

3 oz goat cheese

½ cup dried figs, sliced

2 Tbsp honey

2 Tbsp olive oil

Preheat your oven to 375˚. Arrange your slices of bread on a baking sheet coated with non-stick cooking spray. Spread each slice with goat cheese. Top the toasts with sliced figs and chopped walnuts. Drizzle the toasts with olive oil and honey. Bake for 8-10 minutes, or until golden.

TIP: This toast is about basics: a creamy cheese, a buttery nut, a dried fruit, and honey. Ricotta is a great sub for the goat cheese, and pecans are a wonderful replacement for the walnuts!

Makes 8 slices

BAKED BERRY + MOZZARELLA

I've often made this toast for baby showers, bridal showers, and bachelorettes. It's so feminine! The berries release beautiful hues of pink, red, and purple by baking into the cheese. It is a great bite for any gathering of women. But men, don't be deceived... it's a simple and delicious meal that may become one of your favorites as well! Mild Italian cheeses pair lovely with sweet berries, and along with honey and sea salt, this toast is certain to win you over.

4 slices good bread

1 cup frozen or fresh berries

2-3 oz fresh mozzarella

2 Tbsp raw honey

1 tsp pink Himalayan salt

Preheat your oven to 400˚. Arrange your bread slices on a baking sheet. Spread each with ½ tablespoon raw honey. Arrange your mozzarella slices across the toasts. Top each toast with ¼ cup berries. Sprinkle with a bit of pink salt. Bake for 10-12 minutes, or until the cheese begins to bubble a little and the berries soften.

TIP: If you'd like inspiration for a Christmas toast using reds and greens, top this toast with mint, basil, or rosemary!

Makes 4 slices

THE ELVIS

This is about to get REALLY indulgent. Have you heard of "the Elvis"? It is a sandwich combo of peanut butter, banana, and bacon that is rumored to have been his favorite. As a toast, the Elvis gets even better. We drop one slice of bread and create an open-faced version of this signature, making it into a delicious, finger-licking, messy treat. I make mine on basic sliced sandwich bread, giving this toast a childlike feel with a grown-up take.

2 slices good sandwich bread

3 Tbsp peanut butter

1 banana

2 large slices bacon

Begin by cooking your bacon, either in the oven (400° for 15-20 minutes) or on the stovetop (in a skillet on medium-high heat until crispy). Toast your slices of bread. Spread each toast with 1 ½ tablespoons peanut butter. Slice your banana and arrange evenly among the two toasts. Top with the bacon slices, and dive into the mess.

TIP: For this toast, I love a really delicious, honey roasted, crunchy peanut butter. It adds a bit of sweetness and extra texture that makes this the ultimate treat.

Makes 2 slices

BLACKBERRY JAM + BRIE + BASIL + LEMON

A truth about toast: it never has to be the final draft. It can keep evolving. Often in life, we're encouraged to only share our final drafts. We are told to have things together and put our best face forward. But, I love refining and learning how to be present through it all. We'd never get to a final draft if we were scared to go through the in-between. I love toasts because they're delicious even in their process. They can always get a little better and have more ingredients or flavors. With blackberry jam, Brie, and strong notes of basil and lemon, this toast is wonderful. But perhaps let yourself evolve it a bit, changing up jams and cheeses to find the draft that you like best. Maybe make two, and invite someone into your process.

2 slices good bread

2 oz Brie, sliced

1-2 Tbsp blackberry jam or preserves

2-3 basil leaves, chopped

2 tsp lemon

1 Tbsp honey

Begin by toasting your bread. Spread your toasts liberally with blackberry jam. Arrange your Brie slices over the jam. Top with chopped basil and lemon zest. Then, drizzle each toast with honey.

TIP: To chop basil leaves, stack them on top of one another, then gently roll up like a cigar. Using a sharp knife, thinly slice the leaves until you reach the end of the roll.

Makes 2 slices

ROASTED GRAPE + RICOTTA + THYME

The idea for this toast was birthed after seeing a particularly beautiful food photo. I found the image randomly while perusing Pinterest one afternoon and was immediately intrigued. The luxurious depth of purple coupled with harmonious hues of green caught my eye immediately. Color can do that... it can evoke things within us. Perhaps that is why beautiful food matters so much; it creates both a visual and an emotional reaction. This toast is a simple one, but pulls on color theory and beauty to create both a visually and taste-bud pleasing bite.

4 slices good bread

1 cup red grapes

4-5 sprigs fresh thyme

¼ cup ricotta

Honey, optional

Olive oil to drizzle

Preheat your oven to 400°. Cut your grapes in half and set aside. Spray a baking sheet with non-stick spray and arrange your bread on top. Spread each slice with 1 tablespoon ricotta. Evenly distribute the sliced grapes across the toasts, then drizzle each with a bit of olive oil. Bake for 10-12 minutes, or until the grapes begin to blister and the edges of your toasts are golden. Remove from the oven. Sprinkle with your sprigs of fresh thyme, and if you'd like some extra sweetness, drizzle with honey.

TIP: I like to buy large batches of grapes and freeze them if I can't eat them all before they go bad. Frozen grapes work perfectly fine on this toast - just add a few minutes to the cooking time!

Makes 4 slices

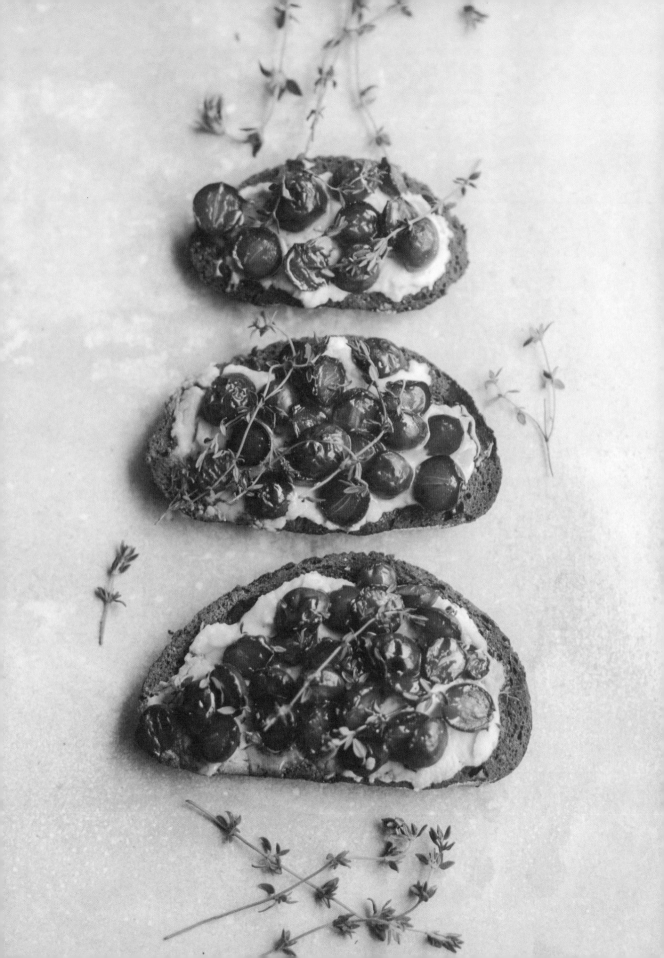

ALMOND BUTTER + BANANA + HEMP SEED

I'm a self proclaimed nut butter enthusiast. I can, and sometimes do, eat it by the spoonful. There is something so satisfying about a velvety, rich scoop of almond butter. And the best part - it's so good for you! It's a great source of protein, fiber, and healthy fats. If I'm having a midday slump and need a bit of a pick-me-up, I like making one of these sweet toasts instead of reaching for a cookie or another sugary fix. Even though it's in the Sweet chapter, it is also a wonderful way to start any morning; almost like having dessert for breakfast.

1 slice good sandwich bread

1-2 Tbsp chunky almond butter

½ banana

1 Tbsp hemp seed

1 tsp cinnamon

Toast your bread. Spread your toast with evenly with the almond butter. Peel your banana half and slice it lengthwise. Arrange the banana slices on top of your almond butter. Sprinkle with hemp seed and cinnamon to finish!

TIP: Bananas and nut butter are a great match. Try varying this toast up with cashew butter, hazelnut butter, or my personal favorite, pecan butter.

Makes 1 slice

RICOTTA + MINT + ALMOND + LEMON + HONEY

Have you heard of the Enneagram? It's a personality assessment that categorizes human behavior into nine types. It is a great tool that helps give language to behavior based on our greatest fears and motivations. The theory is that no personality type is better than another, but each operates differently. I'm a Seven, known as the "Enthusiast". Sevens are notoriously adventurous, spontaneous, and love to try everything. They are often the "yes" friend, because saying no would mean missing out! Sometimes when I create toasts, I see my Seven come to life. I choose to break the rules and keep adding flavors. This recipe is a happenstance of my Seven. It has all the flavors I love, combined into one delicious toast experience.

2 slices good bread

2 Tbsp honey roasted slivered almonds

2 Tbsp ricotta

2-3 tsp lemon zest

1 small handful mint leaves, chopped finely

1 Tbsp honey

Toast your slices of bread. Spread each with 1 tablespoon ricotta. Pile on the roasted almonds, mint, and then top with lemon zest. Drizzle each toast liberally with honey and a sprinkle of lemon juice.

TIP: If you're interested in learning more about the Enneagram, there are so many free tests and resources online. I also wrote an article on it in Issue 19 of Darling Magazine! You can order a copy at darlingmagazine.org.

Makes 2 slices

BLUEBERRY + MINT + LEMON + RICOTTA

Do you know that mint has massive healing properties? It can calm nausea, headaches, indigestion, and even depression. I am fascinated by things that heal. Once, I had a tragic cry with a group of girlfriends. After all of my processing, my dear friend Jess pulled me aside and said, "I just want you to know that I see you." She offered me a compassionate moment of being seen, even though her circumstances differed from mine. She didn't offer advice or a solution, she simply saw. Sometimes in pain, being seen is the ultimate healer. It calms all wounds. With comforting flavors of ricotta, healing properties of mint, and antioxidant-packed blueberries, this is a great toast for a little more healing and a little more calm.

2 slices good bread

¼ cup fresh blueberries

3 Tbsp ricotta

2 tsp lemon zest

1 small handful mint leaves

Preheat your oven to 400˚. On a baking sheet, arrange your two slices of bread. Top each slice with 1 ½ tablespoons ricotta. Add 2 tablespoons blueberries to each toast. Bake for 8-10 minutes, or until the blueberries begin to blister and change color, and the edges of toast are golden. Remove from the oven and top with lemon zest and mint leaves.

TIP: Frozen blueberries work great on this toast as well! I love fresh because they pack in a bit more flavor. But if they're out of season, definitely opt in that bag you have in your freezer!

Makes 2 slices

THANK YOU

My mom used to say, "Show me your friends and I'll show you your future." My relationships have defined me, given me life, and pushed me into a better version of myself. This entire project would have never been possible without the love and support of my people. I stand in unending gratitude.

LINDSEY. You know you deserve all the credit. Thank you for believing in me, for always being a sound board, and for taking toast to town... literally.

COURTNEY. Toodie you're a sister to me who sees potential and the best in people during hard seasons. And even though you don't like bread, thank you for always being willing to bite a toast.

JONNY AND MICHELLE. You have been the ultimate example of marriage. I'm constantly inspired by the way you choose to live, and your talent never ceases to floor me. THANK YOU for saying yes to this and for creating such beauty.

SARAH. Toods remember when you used to ask me to help sort your kitchen? Thank you for believing in my ability, always saying yes to my ideas, and for being a woman who is changing culture. I'm proud to call you a friend.

TO MY SISTER. Snoopy, I think about you often. The way that you're one of the most gifted, yet most humble, people I know. Thank you for always being my confidant and someone who challenges me to think differently. I love you to the moon.

BRIGIT. NOAH. BABIES. You are family. You've taught me what it means to be in intimate, familial, committed relationships. I'm forever changed by your level of freedom. And I stand in gratitude for the introduction to half + half.

Kara Elise is a celebrator who creates experiences that cultivate community. Her love of food was ignited by her love of people. Kara believes that creating intentional time to sit with others is an essential practice, and that beautiful food is the best vehicle to do so. Gathering together in this way gives us a moment to feed our bodies and fill our deepest human desire - to be seen and known.

Her dinner party movement has successfully traveled between the West Coast and London, and continues to grow internationally - drawing in socially savvy, mindful foodies along the way for dinners, retreats, and events. Kara is a 7 on the Enneagram, a very proud ENFP, and the ultimate bubble gum enthusiast.

If you ever find yourself sharing a meal with her, be prepared for table questions - an experience that unearths details about yourself and the people around you. Ultimately, a curated space to share, laugh, and celebrate. For more from Kara, find her at bykaraelise.com, @bykaraelise, and youtube.com/karaelise.